when your teen goes astray

*Help and Hope
from Parents
Who Have
Been There*

JEANETTE GARDNER LITTLETON

Beacon Hill Press of Kansas City
Kansas City, Missouri

10   9   8   7   6   5   4   3   2   1

Contents

Introduction

Like many books, *When Your Teen Goes Astray: Help and Hope from Parents Who Have Been There,* was developed from a need. When our child walked away from our home and our faith, my husband, Mark, and I had no clue what to do. My first inclination was to find other parents who'd been through this.

I was amazed at just how many parents had been in our shoes. I circulated a few e-mails, and within a matter of days, dozens of people were willing to tell their stories and give advice. For more than a year, every time I was in a group of people, in different parts of the nation, I asked if any had been through what I call the "Prodigal Experience." And though I didn't keep formal statistics, I'd estimate that at least 25 percent in each group had experienced this pain.

In this book, you will read the stories these other parents have shared. You will hear from professional family experts as well as recommendations from dozens of unofficial experts. We have changed names and disguised situations at the request of most of these parents, but their godly wisdom is still immeasurable. My whole life has changed as a result of their advice, and I have learned to love our child more than ever.

So, with deep gratitude, I want to thank each person who had a part in this book. I realize it was painful for many of them to share their hearts and be so vulnerable. In some cases it opened wounds that aren't quite healed.

Since we can't list names, they may not receive public acclaim for their wisdom, faith, and encouragement. But I trust that God will bless them abundantly for giving other hurting parents a gift of hope and encouragement.

This book is dedicated to those courageous parents; my husband, Mark; our family and friends who've walked this road with us; Beacon Hill editors Bonnie Perry and Judi Perry, who have a vision for this project; and you, the reader.

If you are enduring the pain of a child who has strayed, all of us who have been involved in this book are rooting for you. We know you're distraught, wiped out emotionally, and maybe even in shock. Make sure you cut yourself some slack. Sit down in your favorite chair with your favorite soft drink, and let the parents in this book offer you comfort and hope. You are not alone. God, your Father, loves you. And He loves your straying child just as much as you do—if not more. For most kids, the prodigal life is a season. Sometimes it's a long season, but you can survive and even thrive.

When Right Kids Go Wrong

"You know . . . I don't have to deal with this. I'm outta' here! And I'm not coming back."

Julie was barely 18, and a senior in high school. Before her parents, Charlotte and John, even realized she had packed, she had scurried out the backdoor—they didn't know who picked her up or where she had gone. Three days later their younger daughter, Katie, broke down into tears and confessed. Julie had called the day before and filled Katie in. She was living with a new boyfriend, one her parents didn't even know about. He wasn't a Christian. In fact, Katie told her parents that none of the young men Julie had been dating for the past year were Christians—Julie had been prompting them on what to tell Charlotte and John so they'd think the boys knew Christ. And now, one of the young men had promised to take Julie away if she got fed up at home.

"We never even saw it coming," Charlotte recalls, thoughtfully biting her lip. "Just a few months earlier she told us she was being called to be a youth worker. She started spending more time learning from her youth leader, and she became the worship leader for her youth group. To encourage her in this, I even took her to a national convention for youth workers—a huge event. She seemed to eat that up, but the next week, she suddenly marched out of the house."

So the teen who was planning a career in youth ministry was now living with a guy. "In only weeks, this teen who'd been so excited about taking chastity vows was facing pregnancy scares," Charlotte says. "And we were in shock."

It's not that Julie was a perfect teen. When she was younger, she'd been a compulsive liar, and Charlotte had caught her starting to lie again. Charlotte didn't liked the friends Julie had been hanging around with and doubted they were the strong Christians Julie claimed. In the six years that Charlotte had been Julie's full-time stepmother, she and Julie had faced many battles, "But many close times too," Charlotte said. And though the battles and rebellion had stepped up a bit lately, they'd also shared some incredible heart-bonding times together.

"Frankly, I thought her behavior problems might be a result of spiritual warfare," Charlotte said. "Since she'd committed her life to serve Christ in ministry, I'd started praying more fervently, feeling that she'd probably face some more intense spiritual warfare to keep her from ministry. But I never, ever, expected her to go off the deep end like this. I never expected to end up the parent of a prodigal child."

Always a Challenge

Some parents have a little more warning than Charlotte and John.

Like Matt and Elise.

"Our oldest daughter has always been what has euphemistically been called 'highly strung,'" Matt says with a hint of a smile. "I remember at 3, she drew blood, biting into my arm when I barred her path out of the car."

As she grew, Christy was definitely a young lady with ideas of her own, but no problems occurred until middle school. "When she was 11, things quickly went downhill," Matt explains. "She was suspended on numerous occasions, and we were called to the school often. At home she still had fits of temper, and we tried all possible methods—the carrot and the stick, withdrawal of privileges, silent treatment, extra attention, careful explanations of actions and consequences, corporal punishment, explanations of how much hurt she was causing us. You name it, we probably tried it."

At one point, Matt, a policeman, received word that Christy, then a young teen, was acting as a child prostitute. The next year, the school reported their suspicions that she was taking drugs. At one point, the teen even attacked her mother with a knife.

As Matt dealt with the day-by-day traumas and tragedies, he reeled in confusion. He reveals a blunt journal entry during that spring in 1999, "It seems that Christy is taking drugs. What do we do? I have no answers. I would like at the moment to see the back of Christy, but then I would be letting her down. I would like to be able to take her in my arms and tell her how much I love her, but then I would be letting her off the hook, and I don't want to do that just yet. I feel she should be punished severely for the way she is pulling our family apart, and I would even like to slap her face. Elise says, and she is right, that this wouldn't help the situation at all. I know that, but I worry because I know if I did that, Christy would be taken away—and that is also what part of me wants. Preferably someone will take her away and then when she is fixed up and 'normal,' we will take her back."

Matt's nightmare continued. Christy pulled her slightly older brother, Daniel, into her circle of friends. Soon Daniel was drinking Christy under the table and joining her friends' drug parties.

"Christy's boyfriend was a nasty bit of work who stole as a

way of life and taught Daniel that there was no point in working for a thing when you can just go and take it," Matt says. The two young men were finally arrested for robbery and sent to juvenile facilities, which Daniel was in and out of for a while.

Meanwhile, Christy became pregnant by her boyfriend. "He beat her so badly that she was in the hospital for three days while she was seven months pregnant," Matt says.

The joy of the impending birth was filled with fear and even more confusion. In his journal, Matt wrote, "My emotions concerning Christy are confusing and leave me in turmoil. I see her as my daughter and love her just for that. I see her as responsible for so much hurt in my house, and I desire to punish her for that. How can we love someone and want to hurt them at the same time?

"At the moment she is not at all well. She was at the hospital yesterday because she was bleeding a lot. It turned out to be the result of an infection, but if she doesn't complete her course of antibiotics, she will do herself serious harm. More than that, her unborn child will also be affected by the toxins that are flowing through her body and that life might be damaged. Father, I pray that You would protect her baby from the abuses that she is putting it through.

"This, too, leaves me with conflicting emotions. I worry for Christy because, despite my best efforts, I still love her. But I am angry with her because if she weren't pregnant, I wouldn't also have to worry about the health of an unborn child. I am angry because she is not taking proper care of herself or the baby. I am angry with her boyfriend for getting her into this mess. I am angry with myself for not being able to be more loving toward Christy. I am scared that something terrible will happen to Christy—that she will go off on her own to have the baby and do herself harm or even die. If she were to do that, then I would feel guilty about being glad she wasn't destroying my family at the moment. I would feel guilty about how little love I have left for her.

"Yet why do I cry? Why do I find myself kneeling beside her bed and weeping prayers to God for her to be safe and well and returned to us undamaged? God, if these are desert times, then I really don't want them to go on for another 40 years. My desire is to know You more and more, but Father, my sanity can't stand 40 years of this."

When the baby was born, Christy was sent to a special program to assess her fitness as a mother. The baby was tagged "at risk" by social services. Anytime she stayed with her family, Christy assaulted her mother and younger sister, and her behavior didn't change with the birth of her own child, so Matt and Elise reluctantly refused to give her shelter or aid. Christy got an apartment and ditched the boyfriend—but started hooking up with a series of men who were even worse.

Meanwhile, Daniel was still doing time for robbery. Matt held the official, heartbreaking, and humiliating responsibility of being the policeman required to take his own son to and from his court hearings.

Christy got pregnant again, and, though she was not even 18 yet, got an abortion without her parents' knowledge. Daniel got out of jail and was allowed to come home with agreed-upon boundaries. Daniel broke the agreement when he brought 12 oz. of speed into the home, and Matt reluctantly called the police—which led to Daniel being arrested again.

The nightmare became worse when the two kids both got involved with hard-core criminals. Matt was attacked outside his home by five masked men, and their home was paint-bombed. Matt and Elise and their younger daughter fled overnight—and still live in temporary accommodations, never knowing what might hit them next.

The Common Problem

These families are only two of the hundreds of thousands of Christian homes—in the United States and around the world —that hope and cope as they begin to face life with a prodigal child each year.

Though Christian counselors and statisticians don't seem to have collected the facts and figures on just how many families face this dilemma, ask nearly any group of Christians how many of them have had to deal with prodigal children, and you'll be surprised at the number who confess to the problem.

We shouldn't be surprised. Prodigal children have been around since the beginning of time. When looking for scriptural examples of prodigal children, we usually point to the story of the prodigal son. However, prodigals have even been prevalent long before then. Consider the first family, Adam and Eve.

Marriage and family counselor H. Norman Wright describes a prodigal as "someone who goes against the family's value system. A prodigal says, 'I'd rather go this way, and I choose to reject all this over here.' In a sense, it's going counter-culture to the way the person has been raised. Prodigals have an *intensity* in their rebellion that is missing in the actions of other highly disobedient kids."[1]

In a sense, Adam and Eve themselves were prodigals, by choosing to go their own way and choosing to reject God's direction. And Adam and Eve were certainly the first human parents to suffer from a prodigal's action, as Cain chose to ignore his upbringing and killed his brother in anger (Gen. 4).

We also find other Old Testament examples of prodigals

and their families: Eli and his sons; David and Absalom; Samson . . .

So if you're a parent who is suffering from the pain, anguish, and confusion of a prodigal child, you're in good company—thousands of people know exactly, or at least pretty much, how you feel.

In the following pages we'll meet some of those people. As we explore some of the main issues parents of prodigal children face, we'll get advice from what others have learned during their journeys. We'll find guidance and support in God's Word—and we'll even look at why God himself sometimes feels far away when we're agonizing over the child He also loves. So if you're at the end of the rope with your child, tie a knot and hang on; hope is on the way.

For Your Reflection

One of the best things we can do when we're facing stress and despair is to write about our thoughts, as Matt did. Consider keeping a journal as you read through this book. At the end of each chapter, we'll give you some questions to help you analyze your own situation.

- Which parents are you most like? Charlotte and John or Matt and Elise? Were you surprised when your child actually crossed the boundary into being a prodigal? What would you pinpoint as that boundary?
- Have you shared Matt's confused mixture of feelings—anger and love at the same time? Write about one of these times when you were battling with more than one emotion.
- What emotion is prevalent when you think about your child?
- If you are married, does your spouse share these feelings?

- Read Gen. 1—3. Imagine God in the role of the prodigal parent here. What emotions do you think He is feeling? If you're feeling especially creative, write a journal entry from God's journal on that day; or read Gen. 4 and write Eve's diary entry.
- Read Ps. 20. Choose a verse to memorize or to write thoughts about.

Empty Beds, Empty Hearts

2

"I thought about going after her, but I didn't," Susan recalls of the night her daughter, Katie, stormed out the door. "I figured her friend Kayla had picked her up and that she would be back in a few hours after she cooled off."

"When I finally realized she wasn't coming home that night, it was too late to call Kayla. And the next day Kayla called me, wondering why Katie hadn't been at school. When I found out where she was, I didn't know what to do. I thought about going to get her and begging her to come home. But she'd been so defiant lately—such a different person. So I thought if I dragged her home, since she'd been so consistently angry, she'd just leave again."

Susan also was aware of Katie's age. Even though Katie was still in high school, she was 18. In the state where they lived, the age of majority for a child is 17. At that age, a child is considered to have legal adult rights for several things, including deciding on living arrangements. So legally the parents and police can't make the child come home.

When Your Child Leaves

Susan and her husband, Andy, aren't alone. According to the Department of Health, more than 1 million kids run away from home each year. The National Runaway Switchboard reports that 86 percent of these runaways are between the ages of 14 and 17, and that 74 percent are females. One in every 7 kids will run away at least once before the age of 18.[2]

The National Center for Missing and Exploited Children (NCMEC) reports that 5 of 10 kids who run away do so because they're tired of living at home. NCMEC says common motivations for running away are:

- Impulsive motivation (tired of living a stereotyped life)
- Drugs
- Alcohol
- Search for new experience
- Need for independence
- Fighting
- Struggles over rules
- Alienation (didn't feel part of the family)
- Forced out of the home
- Peer difficulties[3]

Why do kids leave home? The National Runaway Switchboard reports that more than 40 percent of their callers identify family dynamics as the leading reasons for leaving. Those dynamics include: divorce, remarriage, step or blended families, problems with family rules, discipline, or problems with siblings.[4]

Susan sees Katie in the characteristics on the NCMEC list.

"I guess I shouldn't be surprised," she says. "We'd had a lot of struggles over rules in the previous year or so. And several months after Katie ran away I realized she'd repeatedly dropped hints that she expected to be considered an 'adult' when she turned 18. In my mind, the family rules were being relaxed as Katie showed responsibility. But in her mind, responsibility had nothing to do with it. I was trying to better fulfill her need for independence. But on the other hand, I feel

I was fair and dealing wisely with Katie by letting freedoms come as a result of responsibility. She just couldn't grasp that she had to earn our trust and those freedoms."

As most of us know, teens face many physical changes as their bodies develop and change. This adds stress and confusion to the teenage experience. They're constantly surging with hormones and encountering new feelings both physically and emotionally.

As if that weren't enough, the National Center for Missing and Exploited Children explains that along with the physical changes a teen faces, most teens also strive for personal identity and autonomy. "[For] the runaway, however, attempts to gain independence in a mature, self-sufficient manner fail," the organization reports.[5]

When Katie ran away, it was pretty much for good. But nearly half of teens who run away from home do so more than three times. The NCMEC studied runaways who left home from 1 to 110 times and found that the average age of repeat runaways is age 14. Forty percent of runaways leave home between ages 13 and 15, and another 40 percent leave at age 16 or older. Most remain away from home between one month and one year. Females tend to return home sooner than males, with 3 in 10 teen males staying away from home for more than a year. Older teens tend to stay away longer.[6]

The center also found that teens who leave only once or twice are more likely to claim they ran because they wanted a new experience. Teens who run away more than nine times are more likely to have alcohol as a key factor and are more likely to claim physical abuse as a reason for leaving. About 37 percent of boys and 64 percent of girls calling the National Runaway Switchboard about running away or being homeless also talked of being abused physically and/or sexually.

As with Katie, most runaways make their decisions on the spur of the moment—they are not prepared, have no money, no clothes, and no idea about where to get help. Most have viewed running away as a glamorous act and have no idea of the reality. That's why some experts encourage parents to talk to their teens about how glamorous leaving home seems—and how far from reality that is—when the teen first threatens to run away.

When a teen does take action to the threat and runs away, if you think he or she is involved in drug or gang activity or might be hiding in a bad neighborhood, contact the police and let them investigate the situation instead of getting involved yourself.

"Only go looking for your child in safe areas, but always make sure to have someone at home to answer the phone in case [he or she calls]," explains one police officer. "After you inform the police your child is missing, you should contact family and friends and let them know about your situation."

Parents should also file a missing person's report, make and distribute flyers, and involve the media as much as possible.

When Katie had threatened to run away before, Susan had talked with her about what that meant—about the realism of jobs, of Katie's not even having a driver's license yet, of continuing school. But as Susan discovered, sometimes when kids have made up their minds to leave, they ignore potential pitfalls.

As Susan looks back, she realizes the situation with Katie had probably been building. Besides the expectation of freedom, Susan feels her own attitude might have led to the walk-away. But, she quickly adds, that's not necessarily a wrong thing.

"Over her last couple of years at home, Katie had gotten more and more rebellious," Susan explains. "Though I know it's normal for teens to have mood swings, Katie's were extreme. One minute she'd be the sweetest girl in the world, and then suddenly, literally without warning, she'd be totally ugly with a major attitude. Our family is not a 'fighting' family. My husband is extremely easygoing and just wants to keep the peace, and I'm not far behind him. On the other hand, Katie seemed to enjoy blowing sky-high, and she did so frequently.

"One day I was driving home from work and wondering what stuff might be waiting for me at home that night, since I never knew when Katie would blow. Suddenly, I realized our whole family was walking on eggshells trying not to upset Katie and set her off. She was like a live bomb in a minefield just ready for us to step on it. Katie was running our family with her moods. I decided that had to stop. And I realized I was so busy and emotionally spent always dealing with Katie's moods that I was in a sense neglecting the other kids—our squeaky wheel always got the oil. And our other kids didn't deserve that."

Susan says she girded the strength to stop letting Katie run the family with her tempers. "For some time, that made it worse," Susan explains. "Instead of ignoring the problems, I started meeting them head-on. I stopped trying to coax Katie into good moods. If she wanted to be in a bad mood, I didn't care as long as she took it to her room and didn't destroy the evening for the rest of us. I think maybe when Katie started seeing she couldn't manipulate us with her moods . . . well, I think in a sense that made her give up. I think since she couldn't control us anymore, she may have felt more compelled to follow through on her threat to move out."

Prodigals at Home

Prodigal kids don't always move out, like Dean. "He started making wrong choices at an early age," his mom, Mary, recalls. "As a teenager he began to drink alcohol and smoke marijuana. He never did any of this in front of us, and we were grateful that he never lied when his dad and I confronted him with the evidence. By the time he was in high school, life seemed nearly unbearable at times."

When Dean was out at night, Mary always stayed awake until he came home, praying continually that God would keep him safe. "Now he tells us stories of not knowing how he got home many times, and he says he was sure he arrived home safely because we were praying for him," she says. Dean finished high school only because his parents insisted, and "I threatened to walk him to every class."

Whether a prodigal teen is a runaway or is living at home or is a college-aged student already out of the home when he or she abandons the family values and faith, all three situations are equally difficult for the parents.

All three situations involve the loss of dreams: dreams of who your child would be and his or her commitment to God, success in school (prodigals are notorious for making poor grades!), and easy transition into a fulfilling adulthood. We also must grieve our relationship expectations; most of us don't raise our kids expecting to go through a time when they bring us so much pain, when we don't know how to communicate with them, when we aren't close to them at all.

And it's normal for parents to face emotional and even spiritual anguish. We find new ways to phrase the old "why" question.

Why Do Some Kids Get Offtrack?

Dean was the only one of Mary and Bob's five kids who presented significant challenges. In fact, while Dean was busy running away from God, one of his brothers was running closer *to* God, committing his life to Christ and entering the pastorate.

How can one family, with all kids raised the same way, hold such differences in personal and spiritual acts?

Good question. One most of us prodigal parents wish we could answer. Norman Wright takes a shot from his experience as a counselor. "I believe rebellion comes from a combination of personality, environment, genetics, and the basic sinfulness we all have," he ponders. "Parents might say, 'We raised all of our children the same way. Why is John in trouble and Jane a model child?' But in reality, every child is different. Every child is born into a different family." Wright points out that family dynamics change as more children enter the family and parents react differently to different children. Another dynamic to add is the outside environment that affects the family—job changes, relocation, illness. All such changes can adjust the family atmosphere.

And lest we forget, "Every child has free will," Wright adds. Wright believes that we can find early signs of rebellion in some children. "Some of these signs are found in a child's temperament," Wright explains. "There are children who fall into the category of being oppositional. These kids will challenge authority at every turn. They tend to be negative and stubborn just for the sake of being defiant. There are also children who don't act out their defiance in an aggressive way, but tend to do their own thing or simply ignore what other people want or need."[7]

However, Wright emphasizes that these signs aren't a sure sign that a kid will become a rebel or a prodigal—they're simply clues that what worked for other kids in the family may not work for this child.

Sometimes, in a perverse sort of way, a child's tendency to be a prodigal may be a sign of intrinsic spiritual honesty at the core. Sometimes prodigals are those kids who are searching for God and are challenging spiritual authority in a quest to understand—but just aren't finding the answers. The child may ask questions about faith and not get good answers, may even get trite or phony-sounding answers—and young people are not patient with fakeness. A prodigal teen may be one who senses insincerity or hypocrisy in the lives of people who claim to be Christians.

And what about spiritual warfare? In the first chapter we talked about Julie, who'd committed her life to entering youth ministry and was the youth group's worship leader—and then dove into the deep end of the sin pool. Though Julie's mom, Charlotte, didn't see the exodus coming, in looking back, she had noticed that Julie seemed to be facing more intense temptations in her spiritual life. Several times before Julie ran away, Charlotte had talked with her about those temptations. If spiritual warfare is a real entity in this world, as Scripture reveals, could young people who have great potential to be spiritual leaders face more or stronger temptations to leave the faith than others? Is there a stronger battle raging for their souls?

In his book *Good News About Prodigals,* Tom Bisset says many Christian parents will have at least one child who will drop out of church and active Christian fellowship for a time. He says one survey of pastors and full-time Christian workers revealed that at one time or another in their lives, most had taken either "fairly serious" or "extremely serious" steps to reject their faith.

So Bisset encourages parents with a prodigal child to realize a couple of points. First, rejecting faith is more about searching for truth than about rejecting truth. Second, faith rejection is only one aspect of spiritual change. A person who is rejecting faith is moving and may eventually return to faith. According to Bisset, at least 85 percent of all prodigals eventually come home spiritually and emotionally.[8]

"When Katie decided to leave home, I couldn't help but turn to the story of the prodigal son in the Bible and look at what Scripture tells us of his father," Andy says. "His father probably had a good idea of what was going to happen—after all, most of us have been through many more life experiences than our kids will acknowledge. But he let his son go. He didn't follow his son or chase him down or send his servants to persuade the boy to return. It's the hardest thing in the world, but I guess sometimes we have to just let our kids run. Though I hate it that Katie has chosen this, maybe that's the only way she can find out who she is. And maybe it's the only way she can find out who God is."

For Your Reflection

- Has your child ever talked about running away from home? How did/do you respond?
- If your child has run away from home, write about your first reactions. What were your fears? What were your actions? Was reality as bad as you had imagined it would be? Was it worse or better?
- Let's take a moment to be brutally honest. In your situation, do you feel it would be easier to have your prodigal in the home or out of the home? Why?
- What is the spiritual state of your prodigal? Do you feel any of his or her decisions are a result of intense spiritual warfare?
- Study the story of the prodigal son (Luke 15:11-32). Think of the father. Imagine his feelings and thoughts as the story progresses. Take a shot at writing the story through the father's eyes, as if you are the father living through this.
- Read Ps. 42. Which scriptures speak especially to you in

your situation? Choose one or more scriptures to memorize so the Holy Spirit can minister in your life through them.

Games
People Play

3

"I felt like a failure. Like it was my fault," Ben explains when asked about his first reactions after he realized his daughter had walked away from his faith and his home. "If I'd been a better parent . . . if I'd disciplined her more . . . if I'd spent more time with her . . . if I'd told her I love her more . . ."

Realistically, Ben had spent more time with Courtney than he had with his other four children. She seemed to be a child who needed more time and attention than the others. He'd taken her on date nights and listened to her talk about her day when he got home from work at night. He always treated her with compassion and tried to understand her perspective when she and her stepmother disagreed.

Carol Cymbala, director of the Brooklyn Tabernacle Choir, can relate. When her daughter, Chrissy, decided to step off the straight and narrow, she blamed herself. "I'd think *I'm not a good enough mother*," she recalls. "I always tried to have meals on the table. I always tried to stay home with my three children. But still there were times I couldn't be there. If I left them with a babysitter, which I had to do, I'd feel guilty. I battled often with guilt. So naturally, when Chrissy rebelled, my mind went, *Oh, I should have done this, I should have done that.*"

The Blame Game

When we first realize a child has gone astray, our initial response might be denial or shock. But we can be sure that following right on the heels of that emotion will be the biggee: the blame game. And once that culprit bites us, it's hard to shake off!

Why are we so quick to think we're at fault when our kids have gone off the deep end? There are several reasons, actually.

For so many years we've been responsible for these children. It has been our job to feed them, clothe them, and see that they get good educations. We've been accountable to teach them good manners, respect for authority, and good attitudes.

When we make ourselves answer for these little lives for so many years, sometimes it's hard for us to gradually turn that responsibility over to our kids as they grow.

Sometimes issues are involved like Susan and Katie faced in the previous chapter. Katie wanted more independence; Susan was trying to let her have responsibility, but Katie wasn't taking it. Unlike Susan, some parents forget it's time to let the kids take the reins into their own hands. They may be so afraid their kids are going to mess up that they don't gradually let them grow up. And sometimes it's not fear that keeps us from letting our kids learn responsibility—many times it's so much *easier* for us as parents to go ahead and handle things rather than endure the time and trouble of letting our kids learn. That can sometimes be a factor in the rebellion that the teen chooses to embrace. But there again, the child has made a choice. Not all kids rebel at coddling.

Doin' What Comes Naturally

In the bittersweet and so-realistic movie *Parenthood*, Steve Martin plays a father who is tortured by fears and self-blame when his 10-year-old son is diagnosed with a nervous disorder and a learning disorder. In a pivotal scene, Martin is coaching his son's little league baseball team and makes his son, who's a terrible ball player, play a position no other boy wants to play. When a pop fly comes straight for his son, the boy confidently lines up under the ball. With his son looking in great shape, Martin has a quick fantasy about his son graduating as valedictorian from college, giving a speech that gives all the praise for his self-confidence to his father for making him try things he didn't like—like baseball.

Back in the present, Martin's son misses the ball. The team members complain and make fun of the boy. The child glares at his father and tearfully blames his dad for making him take the position. As Martin leans on the bull pen fence, he fantasizes once again. This time his son is in college, in the top of the campus bell tower, shooting at fellow students and the police. There, the son announces that his behavior stems from his father making him play ball.

All because of one fly ball in one game.

We parents are so susceptible when our kids are concerned. We want to be perfect parents, but we fear in our hearts that we're terrible parents, that everyone else in the world is a better mom and dad than we are. We know in our heads that no one is perfect. However, our hearts just can't quite accept it.

Finger-Pointing

Sometimes we are quick to accept blame for our children's actions because when a child does get into trouble society immediately looks at the parents and says, "What did you do wrong? Weren't you paying attention to your child? Didn't you teach your child better than that?"

The legal system is even beginning to support this attitude. In some states, the powers that be are working at passing legislation making parents responsible by having to pay fines and even serve jail sentences for crimes their kids commit—even when those kids are in their late teens.

And our courts are sometimes inconsistent and illogical. For instance, in some states, the age of majority may be 17 or 18. At the age of majority, a parent has no legal say over what a child does. However, in the same states, a parent can be held responsible for a child's debts until the child is 21.

So while society says, "When your child is 17, you can no longer legally control him or her," it also says, "Well, your kid's 19 and has messed up and incurred debt, so it's your fault and you have to pay."

The attitude of holding parents legally responsible shifts down into our everyday lives quite easily.

Consider the school shootings over the past decade. When the two boys opened fire in Littleton, Colorado, immediately, their parents were censored—especially after incriminating materials were found in their homes. And in the following years, the parents have been sued for huge sums because the parents of the victims hold them responsible for not knowing what was going on in their homes.

As Norm Wright says, "From the outside, it seems like there were some signs that weren't picked up." But he adds, "Of course there are kids who are so secretive that even an involved parent wouldn't see disaster coming."[10]

Take Ben, for example, a devoted, attentive father to Courtney. But Ben wasn't aware until long after the dust settled behind Courtney's runaway feet that she had been pulling the wool over his eyes for months. He wasn't a stupid man, or even necessarily blindly trusting. He just didn't realize his daughter was skilled at manipulation and lying. She had hidden it well.

When the Church Makes the Hurt Worse

It's especially heart-wrenching when other Christians look at us to blame for our children's prodigal choices. And if we're going to be honest, we have to admit that many churches have a very strong, though sometimes subtle, judgment system. Our godly parenting skills are measured by our children's behavior from the time they're very young. People in the church who have not had straying children can be a bit merciless in their snap judgments.

"Goodness! I thought they were a strong Christian family."

"Well, it just goes to show you that even though the parents looked good at church, they obviously weren't consistent and modeling godliness at home."

How can Christians, of all people, be so ugly? Especially those who believe that God gives people free will to reject or follow Him? How can Christians, who are to show their love for God by loving each other, forget to show mercy and understanding and sympathy? How can they forget the old adage, "There but for the grace of God go I"?

Perhaps sometimes the reason involves fear. People like to find a reason for problems. If they can find the cause, they figure, they can prevent the problems from occurring. So, the reasoning is: If a child turns out badly, it's the parents' fault because they weren't good enough Christians. Therefore, if I'm a good Christian, my child won't stray."

Lovely in theory, but oh so wrong!

Sometimes Christians who tend to be judgmental or legalistic live according to formulas, such as the well-worn theory based on Prov. 22:6: If I train up a child in the way he or she should go; when the child is old, he or she will not stray from it.

What is given in the Bible as a general principle is taken as a guaranteed formula. Yes, if we train our children in the faith and teach them God's Word and a love for God, we plant in them materials the Holy Spirit can work with all of their lives, and they probably will follow our faith example.

But because of a sinful world and free will, the promises and principles in the Bible aren't necessarily guarantees. And we fail to acknowledge time frames, such as in this scripture, "Train up a child . . . and when he is old . . . " (Prov. 22:6, KJV). Even this scripture promise doesn't say "Train up a child . . . and all through his life . . . " A lot of variables can happen between childhood and old age.

For instance, several years ago, statistics showed us that baby boomers who had been raised in the faith were returning to the faith after they had children or after they started turning middle-aged. But after childhood, many completely left the faith for 20 or 30 years.

A lot of Christians can't handle the variables and the realization that we live in a sinful world where people have free agency. A world that lacks guarantees is scary for some Christians. Maybe they can't handle a sovereign God who nevertheless allows an imperfect world. And if they admit that "bad kids" can happen to good parents, it adds too many fears to their lives. Maybe they're not ready to struggle with the "why" questions of Christianity (*"Why do bad things happen to good people?" "Why does God allow the innocent to suffer?" "If God is powerful enough to work miracles, why doesn't He always do so?"*).

So sometimes it's so much easier to put the blame on the parents than to face the fear that prodigals happen. And they can happen to any of us at any time. As we read Norm Wright's words in the last chapter, no factors can really predict why a child becomes a prodigal. There's no formulaic answer.

Clinging to the Blame

It's normal to feel blame when our kids go astray. But what about parents who seem to embrace the blame, who will not accept any other reason for their child's failings—who insist they are at fault?

In a sense, perhaps sometimes we *want* it to be our fault. We reason that if we're at fault, if we've done something to make our child act this way, then perhaps we can also do something to make everything right. In a sense, it's a control issue. If we messed it up, we can also correct it—we are in charge.

It's harder for us to acknowledge even to ourselves that this situation is beyond our control; our child has cut the emotional umbilical cord and is now directing his or her own life. That's a scary thing to realize. If it's our fault and we can do something about it, we can possibly make it right and save our child from grief. But if we admit it's our child's choice, then we have to face the fact that we may not be able to do much to help our child, especially if our child lives out our worst nightmares. None of us likes to feel powerless.

Indeed, it is those prodigals, skilled in manipulation and button-pushing, that initiate play in the blame game.

"If you hadn't made me move and leave my friends when I was 13 . . ." "If you hadn't left Dad . . ." "If you hadn't married that man who hates me . . ." "If we had enough money for me to buy the stuff I need to be popular . . ."

Yes, some situations in life can create hardships for kids. Moving can be traumatic. Divorce can be heartrending and destroy security. But most kids survive.

Factors like that may play into a child's rebellion. But plenty of kids go astray who have not dealt with divorce or moves or an unhappy childhood. And plenty of children who go through heartbreaking traumas come out fine. Again, although different factors may come into play, a child makes choices in attitudes and actions. A kid looking for reasons to rebel is sure to find plenty!

When we're staring at the accusing index finger our kids are pointing at us, sometimes we forget that one of the key characteristics of a prodigal is the refusal to be responsible. Even though the kid can run away from us, he or she can't run away from God. A child knows when he or she is living in sin. As the Holy Spirit works through the child's conscience, he or she will naturally look for someone to blame for the problems. And we parents are the easiest targets. If a child admits that he or she is sinning, then that person is faced with knowing he or she has to do something about it. If our kids can point fingers, they figure they're safe. And if we agree with them that we're to blame, they latch on to it.

Dr. James Dobson gives hope to parents of prodigals. He says, "I simply do not believe God intended for the total responsibility for sin in the next generation to fall on the backs of vulnerable parents. When we look at the entire Bible, we find no support for that extreme position." He points out that we see plenty of examples of "rascals" in the Bible—Cain, Joseph's brothers, Samuel's rebellious kids, the prodigal son. But in none of these cases were the parents held accountable for their children's behavior, nor did they—nor did they need to—repent of wrongdoing in relation to their children's behavior.

"It is not my intention to let parents off the hook when they have been slovenly or uncommitted during their child rearing years. . . . Obviously [God] takes our parenting tasks seriously and expects us to do likewise. But He does not intend for us to grovel in guilt for circumstances beyond our control."[11]

Moving Beyond the Blame Game

As long as we're wallowing in blame, we won't be emotionally—or even spiritually—healthy. And actually, when our kids are messed up, isn't it more important than ever that we try to be emotionally and spiritually healthy ourselves? Sick people tend to be weak and unable to do much. Heaven knows in dealing with prodigals we need a great deal of strength, as well as God's grace. If we're going to believe in spiritual warfare, is it too outlandish to believe that Satan doesn't want us to be healthy and at our best spiritually and emotionally? If we're caught in the quagmire of blame, we're probably so focused on our blame that we're not looking to God. We must move beyond the blame game.

Carol Cymbala says, "I've come to this understanding: My parents weren't perfect. But I knew one thing about them without a shadow of a doubt: they loved me. I always felt secure in their love. And even though I haven't been the perfect parent, my children know unequivocally that Jim and I love them and would do anything within our power for them. God used that knowledge to comfort me when the guilt showed up."[12]

A first step is to come before God and ask Him to search our hearts and show us if we have sinned against our children. We can ask Him to forgive us for our failures and to help us move beyond the blame.

When Megan became a prodigal, her mom, Nancy, felt the normal guilt. But when she came before God, she felt that He was showing her a way in which she'd hurt her child. "I realized that I put too much pressure on Megan to be perfect so I would look like a good Christian mother," Nancy admits. "I felt like I had to try harder since my husband was not a Christian. I began to realize I had a tremendous pride that needed to be brought into check."

Nancy had to act on her realization. "I learned that I need-ed to forgive myself. And I also asked Megan for her forgive-ness. She is still not living for the Lord, but she has finally for-given me and we are beginning a new, healthier relationship."

Perhaps when we feel the blame game starting, we should commit it afresh to God. Thank Him that He has forgiven us for any sins and ask Him to help us move forward. James 4:7 does promise us, "Resist the devil, and he will flee from you."

Becoming Healthy, Becoming Whole

As we touched on in the last chapter, when we're parents of prodigals, we need to acknowledge that we're dealing with a loss in our lives. We are grieving people, whether or not we want to be.

"I counsel parents to start [dealing with the emotions of having a prodigal child] by allowing themselves to grieve the loss they're experiencing," Norm Wright explains. "This is a major upset. Your family is not turning out the way you hoped it would and that brings on a whole myriad of emotions—guilt, anger, blame, confusion, and doubt. Those emotions have to be dealt with in order for the family to stay healthy and deal with the crisis in an effective way."[13]

As we begin to realize that we are grieving, our emotions make more sense to us. We realize there's a reason for the unex-pected moods, and we can deal with them more appropriately.

"After Katie left, I'd catch myself going to her nearly empty bedroom and just sitting on the bed," Susan said. "Sometimes I'd just cry. I couldn't have told you why. I thought I was just being crazy. Then one day I saw a parallel between my behav-ior and the way my father would go to the cemetery and sit by my mother's grave and cry. I was grieving the loss of my daughter."

When Susan realized she was grieving, suddenly the tears, the anger, the guilt, the disconnectedness all made sense. And when the emotions of grief struck, it comforted her to know that the emotions were normal.

The advice for people mourning the loss of a loved one through death can also be helpful for people mourning the loss of a prodigal child. Grievers are reminded to eat properly, though they may tend to forget about meals. They're encouraged to get plenty of rest. They're told to let themselves cry if they feel like crying and not to let themselves feel guilty for having negative emotions—that they should just go ahead and vent those emotions in appropriate ways.

Grievers are encouraged to talk. Jenny recommends that parents reach out to others the moment they suspect a child is beginning to struggle or stray. "Pray first. Then have other friends pray," Jenny says. "Find a Moms-in-Touch group to pray with you."

Coming Out of the Prodigal Parent Closet

Of course, sometimes it's not easy to ask people for help. If we admit we have a problem at home, in a sense we feel like we're inviting judgment from those Christians who just don't understand. We may be afraid others will not respect us any-more, as Nancy felt.

When Annie went astray, Diane didn't tell anyone for the longest time. "Annie was a mess," she levels. "She bottomed out at school. I quit my job to stay home because we never knew what Annie might be up to. She had started sneaking out the bedroom window to meet young army men living in a nearby apartment complex. As good parents who had gone through seminary and were in the ministry, we did our best to hide our family problems."

But when Annie ran off with a man Diane suspected was a pimp and halted communication with her family, finally Diane couldn't bear the burden alone anymore. "Her dad wouldn't talk about her at all. But I couldn't keep the problem a secret anymore. Our daughter needed lots of prayer," Diane explains.

Sometimes loving our child *means* telling. It means taking the focus off of ourselves, realizing our child needs prayers more than we need to feel comfortable.

When a parent stops trying to hide the secret that his or her child is a prodigal, sure, a person or two might point fingers and make the parent feel even worse. But something astounding also happens. When you admit you have a prodigal, one by one an amazing percentage of people come to you and say, "I know how you feel. I've been there."

Jim was a missionary when his son became a prodigal. "I was far more concerned with my own reputation for a few weeks than I was concerned for my son," he admits. "But then I repented."

Jim told a community of fellow missionaries about his situation and found that most of them had felt the same kind of shame at some time. "Out of my confession came fellowship and friendship," he says. "Together we found better ways to heal and cope with the situation."

When we admit that we have a prodigal, others generally rush to our aid, providing wonderful healing, power, comfort, and help. We hear their stories of how they dealt with the situation, how God worked miracles, how they coped when God didn't work miracles. God uses all of this information to give us strength and to build our faith. We suddenly feel that we're not alone anymore; we're part of a family. And isn't that what being a Christian is all about?

"Praise be to the God and Father of our Lord Jesus Christ,

the Father of compassion and the God of all comfort, who comforts us in all our troubles, so that we can comfort those in any trouble with the comfort we ourselves have received from God. For just as the sufferings of Christ flow over into our lives, so also through Christ our comfort overflows" (2 Cor. 1:3-5).

For Your Reflection

- How did you feel when you first realized your child was not living out your faith?
- When your child went astray, did you blame yourself? What did you feel you could or should have done differently? Looking back, do you still feel that way?
- Have you ever had a hard time letting go of control of your child, even after he or she became a prodigal?
- How have people responded when they've learned you have a teen who has gone astray? Write about the people who have given you comfort or hope.
- Read Rom. 15:1-7 and 1 Cor. 12. What do these scriptures tell us about how the church should be and how the members of the church should relate to one another? Do you have someone in your life whom you can ask to be your prayer partner about your child's situation?
- Read Ps. 77. Which scriptures speak especially to you in your situation? Choose one or more scriptures to memorize so the Holy Spirit can minister in your life through them.

When Helping Means *Not* Helping

4

"I don't have to put up with this anymore!" Shelly cried as she stormed out of the house. Not until four days later did her parents learn she had moved in with her boyfriend and his roommate. After her parents discovered where she was, Shelly kept a somewhat open relationship with them. But that was almost worse.

"Shelly and I went out to dinner together one night," her mom, Julia, recalls, "and she was talking about how these 24-year-old guys didn't have anything for their apartment. She was very clearly trying to be domestic. We went to some stores and she bought tons of stuff for their apartment—and for their babies who lived with them. I also learned that Shelly was loaning them money left and right and paying their bills."

Shelly didn't have that much money to start with. Still in high school, she had a part-time job and had saved some money from that. However, Julia learned that Shelly had quit her job in a fit of anger over a boss telling her what to do.

Sure enough, within a couple of months after Shelly moved out, she was calling on the phone. "Mark and Damon don't have any money for rent. Can you give us $500? If you don't, we're going to be kicked out on the streets."

Julia and her husband, Samuel, faced the toughest decision they'd ever encountered.

"Now it looks like more of a no-brainer," Samuel says. "But at the time, it was a real struggle. We suspected Shelly was doing drugs with these young men and later learned we were right. Plus, we were afraid if she ended up on the street, she'd end up as a prostitute or something. She'd already made it clear that she wasn't going to come home. We decided giving her the money would be enabling her to continue her behavior. Instead, we just kept inviting her to come home."

Enabling vs. Tough Love

"Enabling" has become a common word in discussing behavior in our society. Enabling is the act of wanting to help someone straighten up, but in the process, actually making it possible for the person to continue unhealthy behaviors.

Enabling our kids can be a financial, physical, or emotional act. For instance, if Samuel and Julia had given Shelly money, as Samuel pointed out, they would have been enabling her— helping her stay away from home and avoid the unpleasant consequences that arose from her behavior. When our kids leave, at some time or another, if they have any contact with us, they will probably want money. Giving them money might enable them to buy drugs or alcohol, or it may help them continue with unhealthy spending habits.

We also enable our kids physically by doing things for them to help them continue in negative behaviors. For instance, if a child defiantly moves away from home without having a car, he or she may face the dilemma of how to get to work and other places. If Mom and Dad still step in and drive the child everywhere, they are actually helping the child remain in an unhealthy situation.

We enable our kids emotionally by doing things like making excuses for them. When a prodigal doesn't show up for work and the boss calls the house, enabling parents make excuses or cover for the child instead of making the child deal with it himself or herself.

The problem with enabling our kids is that while we're saying, "No, I don't approve of your lifestyle," we're giving them what they need to continue in that lifestyle. Although we can love our adult children while not approving of their lifestyles, prodigal behavior is generally self-destructive. By helping our kids keep from drowning in the consequences of their own behavior we're actually helping them destroy themselves in the long run. The sooner they face the consequences of their own actions, the more likely they are to be brought to reality and to the realization that the grass is not as green as it had appeared.

As Samuel and Julia point out, and as you've probably learned, it's not easy to say no to your kids. We parents think that by helping them out "just this once" perhaps we can help them turn around. A parent's heart is torn. But most of the time, the best way we can show love for a child is to "just say no." James Dobson covers this concept extensively in his classic book *Tough Love,* a great source of help and support for parents going through this.

When we love our kids with "tough love" it may involve several components:

Letting Our Children Live with Their Choices

One way we have to show tough love sometimes is by letting our kids live with their own choices. Aubrey recalls that this was one of the hardest things she had to do as the parent of a prodigal son.

"We did impress on Ronnie that he was only hurting himself. And though we were crushed and disappointed by his behavior, we always told him that we loved him and that God loved him too! We told him if he got into trouble that involved the police or jail, we could not or would not bail him out. He would pay the consequences."

Sure enough, one night Ronnie was arrested for drunk driving and ended up in jail. "We appeared with him in court to show our love and support," Aubrey explains. "But the hardest thing we ever had to do was to leave him in jail that day. He tells us now that it was good for him."

As our kids have to face the consequences for their own choices, they often start thinking more about the choices they're making. Unfortunately, it may take the pain and discomfort of living with bad decisions to help our kids begin to wake up, to help them start learning to be responsible.

Unfortunately, we also feel that pain and discomfort. During a support group discussion on letting kids face the consequences for their actions, a woman with a similar situation, Fran, cried out, "I can't stand the thought of my daughter in jail."

The counselor replied, "From what I've heard during the past weeks of what your daughter's been doing, jail will be much safer than a lot of the places she's already been spending nights."

"I realized that what he said was true," Fran says. "That's helped me have peace when I have to watch Shannon go through unpleasant things as a result of what she's done."

When our kids go astray, we ask ourselves, as Samuel and Julianne did, "If I love my child, how can I let him or her end up on the street?"

Tough as it is, maybe instead we should ask ourselves, "If I love my child, how can I *not* let him or her learn that life is all about facing consequences for our actions?"

That's definitely the hard choice for parents to make. In fact, sometimes it's more painful for parents to restrain their power to "make everything right" and watch children go through the tough times. It would often be much easier on us emotionally to bail the kids out. But we have to remind ourselves that then we'd be enabling them to keep avoiding responsibilities and would help them continue on a path to self-destruction.

Let the Child's Problems Be His or Her Own

From the time our children are born (and even before) we are planning for them, protecting them, and helping them. One of our roles as parents is being a problem solver. When our kids are younger, we might tend to solve their problems for them. As they grow older and inch toward independence, we're accustomed to stepping in and helping our kids figure out what to do about difficult situations they face in school and relationships.

Of course, when our kids abandon family and faith, they have no idea the many problems they're bringing on themselves. Their romanticized dreams of freedom from "parental interference" quickly fade into the ashes of real life. Before long, they may be drowning in problems. They might be like Shelly. Not only did she have financial worries she'd never had before, but with her newfound freedom, she was staying up all night partying with her new friends and flunking out of school. Inevitably, relationship problems surfaced with her new roommates and friends and Shelly began to have physical problems too. She wasn't eating well, and because she was now smoking, her asthma was acting up. She was drowning in problems.

"I was so distressed about the things that Shelly was going through," Julia said. "It was affecting my days, and I was often up at night worrying about my daughter. One day at work, I was talking to another woman who'd already been through a similar situation with one of her daughters. She listened sympathetically, and when I asked her advice about how to deal with one of Shelly's problems, she gave me a lifeline that I've clung to ever since then. She pointed out that horrible as it was, Shelly had removed herself from our home and from our role of actively parenting her. She said, 'For right now, unless Shelly decides to come home and let you parent her again, you're moving into a new role as a parent. You're going to have to let Shelly be the adult she wants to be, and you're just going to have to step back and encourage her as a parent encourages an adult child. That means letting Shelly figure out how to deal with her own problems instead of trying to fix everything for her.'"

"That was so freeing for me," Julia recalls. Julia still let Shelly talk to her about the problems but now limited herself to offering sympathy. She says, "I remember so many times just telling Shelly things like, 'Yeah, it's tough having bills due every month, isn't it?' or 'Don't you just hate some of the worries that come with being grown up!'"

That doesn't mean parents can't make suggestions or offer advice. But for a while, if your child has moved out, your parenting role must adjust. You must think of yourself more in the role of a friend than of the parent you've been to that child for so long. After all, how would you treat a friend? You would sympathize with a friend and you might give advice, but if you have a healthy personality, you won't take responsibility for your friend's problems.

Learning to let a child's problems be his or her own is easiest when the child is living away and has severed the relationship for the moment. Then, although the break in the relationship is distressing, the parent doesn't usually see the problems and doesn't have to deal with the temptation to step in. It's a little tougher not to step in when the child is not living at home but is still in communication with the parents. When the child still lives at home, we may be in even more of a difficult situation. Learning to let a child's problems be his or her own might mean making the child be responsible. For instance, if your son is supposed to be at work at 7 A.M. and is supposed to get himself up, but ignores his alarm, you may need to refrain from waking him, if he hasn't asked you to do so. Then let him deal with the problems caused by being late to work. At that stage, maybe he'll ask you if you'll awaken him. If you choose to do so, fine. But help him learn responsibility by waking him and going on with your life—not hovering over him, nagging until he finally gets up, as you would with a younger child.

Or if your daughter has come home with alcohol on her breath when the house rules are "No drinking or no driving," you may need to take away the keys and let her figure out how she's going to get to the places she needs or wants to go. Don't rush in to give her rides everywhere because then you're solving the problem she's created. Let her deal with the problems brought about by the consequences of her choices. In such a case, having to ride the bus for a few days instead of driving to school as she normally does can make a world of difference!

The Guilt Trip of Being "Jesus"

For families of faith, sometimes the emotional issues with prodigal kids can be exacerbated by our spirituality. For instance, while Shelly was gone, Julia was very concerned about "being Jesus" to her daughter.

"A Christian is to be giving and forgiving," Julia explains. "I'm not sure what impetus started the guilt trip. But I began thinking, *How could I give to people outside our home, but not give financially to our daughter?* I wanted to be a good reflection of Christianity for our daughter. I wondered if perhaps I shouldn't be playing the heavy so much. I thought about WWJD—what would Jesus do? I thought about the grace God shows us and how He loves us and pursues us unendingly. And I began to wonder if I should do just anything and show un-limited grace to bring Shelly back home."

Thankfully, Julia discussed the thoughts with a good friend. "She told me, 'Look, I know you guys. You've raised Shelly in the church. You've helped her study her Bible. You've taught her scriptures and have constantly shared your faith with her. You've shown her grace countless times while she was at home, and you've still been there for her. Shelly has already seen Christ in your life.' She emphasized that it wasn't a matter of Shelly not knowing what was right; Shelly knew about God and His grace and mercy. She basically pointed out that by giving in to Shelly's demands in the name of 'grace,' we'd be playing the suckers. Samuel and I wouldn't be helping Shelly grow or learn anything spiritually but would be enabling her."

We want to be good parents; we want to be godly examples. As there is a time for grace, there's also a time for tough love in Christianity. If we believe in spiritual warfare, and if we believe Satan is battling for our kids, then he wants them to self-de-struct. Saying no to our kids now with the hope that they will return home later, as the prodigal son did, might be the most godly thing we can do. After all, it must have broken the first Parent's own heart as He sent Adam and Eve out of the garden. But after the two sinned, God had to practice tough love by letting His children face the consequences of their actions. The time for grace would come later.

Likewise, as we have to show tough love and let our kids face the consequences and problems they've brought on, we can cling to the hope that the time for grace and the fatted calf may come later. As we hold out and make our kids face the consequences for their actions here on earth, we will also be giving them the picture of a spiritual reality. The grim reality of Rom. 6:23 tells us, "The wages [consequences] of sin is death," and Scripture informs us that what we sow, we'll reap (Gal. 6:7). As our kids face earthly consequences, they're much more likely to start thinking of eternal consequences of their actions. While Scripture tells us that God is love (1 John 4:8), it also shows us examples of God's boundaries.

How to Explain This to Kids

OK, so you've decided to make your child face the consequences of his or her own actions and to let the child face the problems he or she has created. Making the decision is one of the toughest things you'll do. Now you'll face more challenges —telling your child.

Unfortunately, there aren't any magic words. All you can do is explain it the best you can. Try to explain your reasoning and reaffirm your love for your child. It's tempting sometimes, even for parents, to show their own hurt with a "you made your bed, now you have to lie in it" attitude. While that may be straightforward, it's usually unproductive. A sympathetic, loving approach is usually best, "I realize you're an adult now, and I respect you too much to step in and try to solve your problems for you." With that attitude you're going back to the old successful-communication philosophy of making "I statements" instead of the accusing "you" statements.

You may find your children to be more like toddlers at this stage, though, no matter what approach you take! Toddlers, no matter how much you explain, can't accept reason. Often, neither can kids who've gone astray. Depending on their personalities, they're probably too focused on what they want to understand or accept. After all, most prodigals tend to be at a somewhat selfish stage in their lives, only thinking of themselves and what they want.

And like toddlers, your kids may respond with all sorts of emotions.

You might face anger. "I hate you. I'll always hate you!"

You will probably face blame or a guilt trip, "I can't believe you're not going to help me! It'll be your fault!"

Kids might try emotional blackmail, "If you don't help me out, I won't graduate. If you want me to graduate, you'd better give me the rent money I need."

Some will wheedle or try to pull you into an argument or try to manipulate you. Maybe your child will ask again and again, like a toddler trying to wear you out and wear you down until he or she gets his or her way.

By knowing your child, you probably have a pretty good idea of what to expect. Chances are, you will face an emotional battle. So nothing is wrong with preparing yourself emotionally and spiritually.

You might find it easiest to set up a time to talk with your child about just what you will and will not do to help him or her while he or she is going through this phase. This might open the conduits for communication better than just catching your child off guard sometime.

You also might make sure you plan a time when you and your spouse can talk to the prodigal together. After all, kids are famous from the time they're tiny for mastering the "divide and conquer" scheme. Your words will pack more of a punch if you're standing together. One woman, Ellen, had such problems with her manipulative daughter playing her and her husband off each other separately, that Ellen had her husband start listening on the telephone line anytime she was on the phone with their daughter. So approaching your child together will help you avoid misunderstanding later. You might also decide ahead of time that one of you will be the main speaker and one of you will be the main praying partner.

When dealing with your child as a duo, you might find it a wise move to "role play" the situation with a friend or spouse first, especially a friend who knows your child. You try to explain your thoughts and feelings as if you're talking to your child and let your friend respond in different ways your child might respond. This can help prepare you for the different scenarios, can help you learn to articulate your feelings, and can help you be stronger emotionally.

Ask others who've been in your situation for advice on how to deal with this, specifically, words they've found successful. And ask others to pray for you when you talk to your child about this. You need the power of prayer—not just for your child but for your own spiritual battle and emotions as you try to show tough love.

When It's Appropriate to Step In

While it's best to let your prodigal learn the consequences of choices, at times it is appropriate to step in. But make sure you have good reasons for doing so.

For instance, nearly a year after Shelly moved away from home, she was in trouble again. She'd asked for money several times over the year, and Julia and Samuel had stood firm, still feeling Shelly was not taking responsibility for her actions. But this time she'd tried to duck out on a lease. The apartment complex went after her. Shelly needed to raise $1,500 or be evicted.

"I just knew if she was evicted, she would move in with us, and that wouldn't be a good scenario," Julia recalls. "She would still have to pay $600 a month for her apartment until the end of the lease, even if she was evicted. And on top of her other bills, I knew she'd expect to get by without paying us rent—

which would not be helping her learn to be responsible. I could just see too many negative potential outcomes."

Samuel could foresee negative potential outcomes too. And before Julia even mentioned her concerns to Samuel, he'd already made up his mind.

"I decided in this case to take the money out of savings and loan it to her," Samuel says. "We were going through a tough time ourselves, so it's not like we had this extra money at hand. But I really didn't think she should move back home. I felt that would bring nothing but trouble for our family. And frankly, it was worth the money not to deal with the hassle."

Notice that while Samuel and Julia stepped in to help Shelly out, they still set boundaries. One boundary they set was on how much upset they'd let their family face. While Shelly was living at home, the family was in constant turmoil because Shelly liked fighting. Samuel and Julia and their other kids were enjoying the peace that came into the home after Shelly left and were reluctant to step back into making their home a battle zone. So Samuel and Julia decided setting the boundary of protecting their family's peace was a priority.

Rather than just giving Shelly the money ahead of time, Samuel and Julia let Shelly go to court first, to see if she could set up a payment system with the judge. Samuel went to court with her to support her, but he made Shelly face the emotional consequences of standing before lawyers and a judge.

Although Samuel and Julia helped Shelly, they did not give her the money; they gave her a loan. Samuel set up a payment schedule. And though Julia hated seeing Shelly have to get a second job to make those payments, they let Shelly live with that consequence. When making a formal loan to a child, set up the situation as professionally as you can. Draw up documents to be signed.

Keep the overall picture in mind. Take the steps that will work out best for everyone involved, and do what you can to keep helping your child take responsibility for his or her own life.

Knowing when and how much to help your child is never easy—especially when you're caught up in the emotion of the moment. So never feel embarrassed to get professional help and advice from people who've been there. Most of all, remember that God knows the pain of a parent who has to say, "I'm sorry, but I have to say no, even if it means letting you suffer." Let Him soothe and comfort you as you practice the tough love of parenting.

For Your Reflection

- In your situation, what does enabling your child look like? What are you tempted to do that would help your child continue in negative behaviors?

- What are some examples of ways you need to practice tough love or have learned to practice it already?

- How does your spouse feel about enabling and tough love? If this is a new concept for your spouse, or one he or she doesn't feel ready to accept, how can you explain it?

- What are some boundaries you've set in place in your life since your teen went astray? What boundaries have you set in your family? in your marriage? What other boundaries do you need to set? How can these offer protection to you and others involved, including your child?

- Read Mark 12:29-32. Some Christian leaders say we have to love ourselves before we can love others as ourselves. How does setting boundaries display love for God? for the people God created?

Talking to the Stranger in the House

5

"'My friend and I were picked up for shoplifting yesterday,' my daughter told me the morning after her 13th birthday," Cassandra recalls. "Dayna stood leaning against the bathroom doorjamb. Her dad was at work, her sister was still in bed, and her brother was talking to his gerbil instead of getting ready for school. I was standing in front of the bathroom mirror getting my hair ready, and I remember looking in the mirror and seeing the shock on my face reflecting back at me. I wondered how our beautiful daughter, the one called to the mission field, could turn into a thief overnight."

As far as Cassandra knew, the trouble Dayna got into kept her from making shoplifting a regular habit. But Cassandra still realized that Dayna had changed. "A real stubborn attitude surfaced from within her. She still did what we said, but her attitude changed from the missionary-minded kid to an unpleasant kid I didn't know."

What happens when we feel a child has turned from an angel to evil incarnate, seemingly overnight? Suddenly it seems like you're living with a stranger. "It was as if she was another human being. She wasn't the daughter I raised," says Carol Cymbala of her daughter, Chrissy.[14]

So how do we communicate with this unfamiliar person in our child's familiar body?

Rodney Gage, author of *Why Your Kids Do What They Do,* and Miles McPherson, author of *Parenting the Wild Child,* both recommend that we look at some of the forces behind our teens' behaviors.

If changes occur during the early teen years and aren't too extreme, some of the attitudes and actions may be more consistent with changing hormones than actual rebellion. After all, during the teen years, a person's whole body changes. Along with the physical changes, the teen's whole universe changes.

During the teen years, because of hormones and the natural need to start asserting themselves, teens often start withdrawing from parents and seeking their own independence. Peers start having a stronger influence in their lives. Sometimes, as they change emotionally and physically, teens truly don't realize how they come across. They don't realize their tone of voice is becoming disrespectful or that their faces may reflect attitudes they don't really feel. Teens haven't yet learned the social skills, diplomacy, or communication tips that adults have learned.

Teens also face natural spiritual crisis. They transition from a grade-schooler's precious prayers and automatic trust in Jesus to questioning and even arguing about their faith and morals. Again, they may not be rebelling or running away from their faith. They may just be trying to make sense of Christianity and find out what the faith your family has practiced means to them personally.

Accordingly, Gage, McPherson, and other youth experts advise that parents give several ounces of grace to teens when gauging their attitudes and behaviors. Try to analyze if your teen is dealing with hormones or showing true signs of defiant rebellion.

Stuart became a prodigal during his final years of high school. As Ron and Kim dealt with their son's behavior, Kim also kept an eye on Robin, who was just entering her teen years. When Robin started to respond to her parents rather rudely at times, Kim started praying desperately that Robin would not follow the footsteps of her older brother. Finally, one day when Robin was acting disrespectful, Kim observed, "Robin, I don't like the tone in your voice. Do you mean to sound so ugly? Is this an attitude problem, or are you worried about something?"

Robin looked at her mother in genuine surprise. She'd had no idea how she was coming across. Kim's honesty opened new doors of communication with Robin. And it also helped Robin start learning how to express her feelings appropriately.

The same kind of honest communication can help us help our teens when they face questions of faith. When a child asks something like, "If God is so good, why are innocent people suffering?" we're often tempted to panic, thinking our child is going to become a spiritual prodigal. We may rattle off, "We just have to trust God. You'd better learn now just to trust God." We catch ourselves becoming a bit defensive, especially when they ask the tough questions that expert theologians wrestle with! We don't want to show our own ignorance or lack of doubt with teens.

Instead of feeling threatened by a teen's struggle with faith and moral issues, parents can learn to use these as a stepping-stone for great discussions. Remember that we don't have to have all the answers. The Holy Spirit will work in our teens' lives (even without us). When we counter our teens' questions or comments with other questions like, "That's a good question. Why do you think God lets the innocent suffer?" During the conversation, teens will open to you the doors of their hearts, minds, and spirits. As you let them verbally wrestle with their questions, they'll also start listening to the conclusions you've drawn in your spiritual life. And it's even a great time to help them see how the Bible can have answers for these questions and for their lives.

Even when we don't have answers, that is reassuring for our teens. They may feel helpless and hopeless when they don't find easy answers to their spiritual questions. They may give up because spirituality seems too overwhelming. But if they realize an adult is also struggling with questions, they can take hope that it's normal.

However, don't just use your "I don't know" as an excuse to allow a teen to struggle alone. Instead of leaving the child frustrated, do a little bit of homework. Find the resources to help your teen find the answers, or choose to examine potential answers together.

When It's More than Teen Angst

What do we do when we look at our teens' behaviors and realize that we can't write this one off to hormones, that they are definitely being defiant and rebellious?

When we realize our child has changed and he or she suddenly starts plying us with attitudes and ugliness that we haven't encountered before, it can throw us for a loop. But at a certain point we have to admit this is more than general teen angst. Let's look at some suggestions of what to do when we're afraid the teen we love has morphed into something unrecognizable.

1. Confront Quickly

Who has the time or energy to deal with the conflict a rebellious child can bring into the home? Depending on our personalities, we may be tempted to ignore the problem in hopes that it will go away. But defiance is like a wound. Often if we ignore it, it doesn't heal; it becomes infected and festers. So some specialists advise us to confront our kids quickly—as soon as we realize the behavior is truly defiance.

As we confront, we can remember a couple of communication tips:

- Confront the behavior without condemning the child. It's tempting to say, "You've become a nightmare to live with." Instead, it's best if we bite our tongues, pray for diplomacy, and carefully let the child know, "I don't like this attitude I'm seeing. Is something wrong? It's not like you."

- As mentioned in the last chapter, use the good old "I" statements. "I'm disturbed by this lack of respect I'm seeing," even if "You're really becoming a brat" seems more direct. "You" sentences come out as too accusing, which automatically puts a wall between you and your child.

Sometimes kids start showing prodigal behavior when their natural desire for independence runs amok. If you feel a need for control or independence is part of the problem, you can help your teen by giving him or her choices, or phrasing your words as choices. During a confrontation, if you start to lose control, get space. Call for a time out and, like wrestlers, go into your separate corners to cool off before trying to logically resume the conversation. Say something like, "You know, I'm too upset right now and I'm afraid I am not thinking clearly or may say something I'm not sure I really mean. Let's pick up the conversation again later."

Of course, that's often easier said than done. Parents aren't perfect. God is still working in our lives too. And prodigals have a way of knowing exactly how to push all of our buttons.

Sometimes they even take great joy in doing so! After all, if they can get us to act on their level, or they can affect our days, they feel they've won a victory. And much of being a prodigal is about power. We have to remember, power has been the impetus for sin from the beginning. Consider Lucifer's power struggle with God!

Often prodigals are what Norm Wright calls an "Oppositional Personality." Their actual goal is to make us miserable. In such cases, if we can learn not to give our kids the emotional power they crave, we not only keep our sanity more intact but also keep control of the situation ourselves.

Other counselors also recommend that we honestly look at our own lives and see if the power struggle is worth it. Do we really have to hold on to power in this situation? Or are we only doing so for our egos?

If we are battling for a moral or developmental issue, that's one thing. If we're holding on to the fight just to prove we're still boss, that's another. Should that be the case, sometimes we can graciously say, "You know, I didn't realize it's so important to you to have purple hair. Since it's not a moral issue, I guess I don't care what color your hair is after all."

Sometimes it goes back to the old adage of choosing our battles. It's easy to become so paranoid that we're always suspicious of our prodigals and expecting the worst. After all, they've shocked us, hurt us, and we never know when they're going to ambush us with more pain. We'll tend to be defiant ourselves about any issue they bring up. But we need to keep looking at the battles individually instead of lumping them all into an automatic call to arms. Letting our prodigals win a battle here and there may help us keep communication lines open with our teens.

Letting go of the battles that aren't really important also

helps us keep on track as parents, leaving our energy for the battles that *are* really important to us.

When we have to talk to teens about issues that we know are going to be battles, we need to let our kids know the reasons behind our actions, if only to model reasoning.

2. Confront the Lifestyle

Confronting behaviors while the child is at home is one thing. Parents also deal with the decision on whether or not to confront the prodigal's overall lifestyle.

Jon faced this dilemma when Stacy suddenly threw her morals to the wind and ran away from home. On one hand, Jon knew that Stacy knew better. She had been raised in the church, and the family had practiced their faith at home. She knew that what she was doing was sin. What good would talking about it do?

But he also realized that he felt a need to talk to his daughter to try to persuade her to change before she got too immersed in behaviors that would totally destroy her future.

Jon invited his daughter to come over and sit down with him one night. He talked to her as lovingly as he knew how. He didn't beat her over the head with the Bible but shared scriptures and emphasized how much God and he loved her and said he wanted to make sure she knew where taking drugs and having promiscuous sex might take her.

Jon presented his case with absolute diplomacy, following all the good communication tips the experts give us. He used "I" statements, he tried to draw her into conversation, he reaffirmed his love, he kept his temper.

Stacy folded her arms and tightened her lips. Her eyes hardened and refused to meet Jon's pleading ones. His words seemingly fell on deaf ears.

Was his confrontation a failure since it didn't bring a tearful, repentant scene?

Not at all. Jon needed to express his feelings for his own sanity. Sure, communication is usually a two-way street; its success is measured not only by information given but also by information received. But sometimes you just have to talk to what seems to be a brick wall. Besides, we never know what little thoughts will get through the tiny chinks in a wall. We may not see an outward response to our messages, but the Holy Spirit will use little bits of our words in our children's lives.

Sure, your prodigal knows that what he or she is doing is wrong and is against everything you feel passionate about. But feel free to confront it anyway. You need that. Try to practice good communication tips. But even if you lose your temper or feel frustration, forgive yourself. Your caring enough to confront your child will speak volumes.

You may also need to confront the prodigal later in your relationship. Stacy had always been good at getting her way, but when she went astray, she became entirely self-focused and became a manipulation master. She started trying to work her mom, Susan, and Jon like a pro. Of course they saw right through it. Finally, Susan was straight with Stacy, "Look, you're playing games. We know what you're doing, so it's not like you're pulling the wool over our eyes."

Again, Susan's words fell somewhat on deaf ears to all appearances. Stacy, of course, denied that she was doing any such thing. But Susan had put the cards on the table. Later she could say, "Stacy, I feel like you're trying to manipulate us." Stacy would deny it, but back off on the behavior. It was much easier for Susan than subtly trying to get the point across or wordlessly fight the manipulation.

3. When You Can't Confront

Some parents find their prodigals resist hearing anything. "I just knew Phil was going to become a preacher when he grew up," Angela recalls with a smile. "Like our other kids, he grew up in church. Every time the doors were open, we were there. He heard the message of Christ loudly, clearly, and often. Phil was a lovable kid and sang in the choir. He spoke at youth Sunday every year and did a great job. He had such a sweet spirit."

But then Phil went to college. "For the first couple of years he was faithful to God, but then something turned his heart cold." Now Phil becomes furious anytime his parents try to talk to him about faith or about his new, drug-laden lifestyle.

What do you do when your child refuses to have that confrontation you need? Drop it and ask God for the grace to live without the verbal confrontation. Even a refusal to discuss the matter shows you that your prodigal feels conviction. Find another constructive way to take care of your need to express your feelings. You may want to write a letter. If you send it, realize, however, that your child may not read it or may never respond. You may just want to write the words and destroy the letter or leave it on your computer.

This is another situation in which role-playing may help. Ask a dear friend or your spouse to sit in a chair and "be" your child while you express what you'd like to tell your child. Or, be like JoAnn when she felt a need to confront. She just sat across from an empty chair and spoke as if her child were sitting in that chair. This helped her release her feelings so she could move ahead.

Moving On from There

The most important thing to do when a child goes astray is to try to keep communication lines open. That may mean swallowing our pride or working at forgiving our children for the pain they have brought us. Rom. 12:18 tells us, "If it is possible, as far as it depends on you, live at peace with everyone." Most of the time it's up to us to take the first steps of reconciliation, if need be, and to work at a relationship with our prodigals.

That doesn't mean we don't need space sometimes. After Jon confronted Stacy, he just couldn't talk to her for a while. It hurt too much and he was too afraid of what he might say. But eventually, he began to work at communication.

Although we need to be willing to take the first step in communication, we do need to be sensitive to our children. Sometimes they need some space too. Cara relentlessly pursued Scott when he left her home, his morals, and the faith he'd been raised in. Scott didn't return Cara's calls and definitely displayed resentment and anger when she would show up unannounced. Cara was just trying to stay close to her son, but her son needed some space. Cara finally realized this and left Scott alone for a while. Within a few weeks, she secretly was pleased when Scott started opening the communication doors again.

Often communicating with prodigals is like building a whole new relationship. We may not be able to communicate with our child on the same level we did before. So that may mean letting go of some expectations, as painful as that may be. Our relationship has changed, so we have to become acquainted with where the new relationship is.

After our child has become a prodigal, it colors our whole way of viewing that person we love. We may suddenly be on edge and only see the child through "prodigal-colored glasses."

When you look at your child, don't let everything you see be colored by your disapproval of his or her current behaviors and lifestyle. Try to look beyond the negatives that distress you. One of the difficulties of loving a prodigal is seeing the child you have always loved in the middle of the "monster." Look beyond the negatives and focus on the positives. This will help your attitude toward the teen. And comment on the good qualities. Praise your child for what you *can* praise him or her for. This will speak volumes.

Jon found that one result of his confronting Stacy initially was that he was able to move on from there. He was able to bite his lip when Stacy's behavior drove him crazy. Like Jon, we have to learn to refrain from repeated lecturing or scolding. If we keep scolding our wayward teen, not only will our words probably ring hollow, but they will prove detrimental to our children. If prodigals are making an effort to improve their behavior, they may feel our scolding is a reminder that they're worthless. They may give up. But any kind of change in their lives—even if it seems behavior-based rather than a change from the inside out—may indicate that God is moving in their lives. So refrain from the scolding.

What do you talk about when you don't know what to say to this child? Look for the nonthreatening, "safe" subjects on which to communicate, and you'll soon find your grounding.

Setting Communication Boundaries

Karen worked hard to reestablish communication lines with Sandi. The two had always been close before Sandi "lost her senses," as Karen called it. As they moved ahead in their relationship, Karen was delighted that things seemed to be just like old times.

But unfortunately, she was quickly reminded some things don't change easily. Always one to share everything with her mom, Sandi started talking to Karen about the parties, getting drunk and high, or about her lovers. Karen realized that Sandi wasn't trying to hurt her or shock her or prove a point. Sandi was just prattling on about everything as she'd always done. Karen was freaking out inside but was afraid if she said anything, she'd destroy their communication.

Some parents are OK with this kind of thing. It helps them to know exactly what is going on so they can wisely help or pray. Other parents, like Karen, can't deal with it. It hurts too much or gives them too much of a temptation to nag. And that's OK too.

What does a parent do in such a scenario? As we mentioned in the last chapter, setting boundaries is an important part of dealing with your child. Not only do boundaries protect your prodigal, but they also protect you, the parent. And you need and deserve that protection. God doesn't expect you to be a doormat, even in the area of communication. He doesn't expect you to put up with everything in the name of love.

So feel free to tell your child, "Whoa, I love you, but it distresses me to hear the details of what you're doing." Be honest with your child. Karen could tell Sandi something like, "Sandi, I know you know I disagree with your lifestyle right now. And I know you don't want me nagging you about it. But if you tell me about smoking pot, you know as your mom who loves you, I have to speak up and tell you about the dangers of it. So if you don't tell me details about the stuff you're doing, I won't lecture you."

Your boundaries may lie with not hearing anything your child is into, being open to anything he or she says, or falling somewhere in between. Your boundaries also may depend on why your child is telling you these things.

Andi could listen to a little more than Karen could. Her daughter, Shawna, often talked about her live-in boyfriend. Andi didn't let Shawna go into sexual details, but Andi had always talked to Shawna about her boyfriends. And she practiced the same procedure now. She'd ask Shawna what she liked about the guy. If Shawna thoughtlessly slipped into bedroom talk, Andi clearly, tactfully changed the subject.

However, when Andi's son, Keith, came home from college announcing that he was gay, Andi responded differently. She was distressed that Shawna was living with a guy. But she was totally repulsed by Keith's revelation. She couldn't respond like she did with Shawna. She tactfully tried to draw back when Keith started chatting about his boyfriend, just as he'd always chatted about his girlfriends. When Andi didn't want to hear about it, Keith charged her with not accepting him. "If you really love me you'd accept that I'm gay and deal with it," he shot at her.

Andi loved her son and realized she had to let go of him to live his own life—right or wrong—as she had Shawna. But Andi had to set a boundary with Keith that she didn't set with Shawna. She just could not discuss his boyfriends with him. She had to tell him, "Keith, I love you. You know that. You also know this behavior is destructive. It will hurt you emotionally and spiritually and could kill you physically. So I'm sorry, but at this stage in my life, I just can't hear you talking about this."

And that's OK. Keith didn't understand. But that's OK too. Parents have to protect themselves and do what they think is right. Even when other parents with prodigals don't set the same boundaries, parents have to do what they feel comfortable with. Even if Keith hadn't been a bit defiant with his "love me, love my lifestyle" attitude, and even if he was hurt by Andi's stance, sometimes parents have to realize it's the best of two evils for them personally if they make boundaries for themselves, even if the kids don't understand.

Set Communication Protections

Just as we sometimes need to set boundaries in our communication relationships with our kids, sometimes we need to think about the steps we need to take to protect ourselves. Peter was horrified when Andrea moved out in a huff. He was distraught with his oldest daughter's behavior. He still felt the grief a week later when Andrea showed up at the house to move out her belongings, bringing a couple of seedy-looking guys with her. Peter hardly said anything to his daughter. Part of the reason he held his tongue was because he was afraid he'd say too much. He was especially afraid of losing his temper and saying something he shouldn't in front of Andrea's friends. He waited to talk to his daughter about the issue until he had no witnesses to misconstrue his words.

On the other hand, Lisa wanted witnesses when she had to deal with her daughter Kimberly.

"Once Kimberly threw her conscience to the wind, she became so deceptive," Joyce recalls. "I'd talk to her about something unimportant and later I'd learn that Kimberly had given a report to her father about the conversation that was completely inaccurate and totally unfair. I learned to try to make sure I initiated any conversations with Kimberly around a third party, my husband or other daughter. I told my husband I was doing this. And I asked my daughter to keep an ear on our conversation to let me know if I'd been unclear on something.

"Also, every time I talked to Kimberly on the phone, I tried to make sure I was on an extension that was near my husband. That helped my husband see that Kimberly wasn't always being honest with him about what I said and did. That protected me and my integrity as well as my relationship with my husband, especially during the early days when my husband had a hard time accepting the fact that Kimberly had become a prodigal."

Making the Difference for Your Child

Trina dropped out of school and moved in with her boyfriend when she was only 16. To make tough matters tougher, the boyfriend was abusive. Trina plunged into a lifestyle filled with a wild, cruel bunch of drug addicts and a psychotic boyfriend who frequently beat her and tore down every bit of confidence she had. Trina's life was filled with problems she'd brought on herself.

Trina's mom, Eileen, agonized over her daughter. She realized that Trina was reaping the consequences of her actions. But she also felt compassion in her soul for this child she loved so dearly. "The world was beating Trina up nonstop," Eileen says. "Trina knew her actions were wrong. She knew she'd gotten herself into this pickle. So I felt my role was to be her supporter. I tried to build her up, to help restore her confidence, hoping someday she would leave the jerk. Every time I saw her, I focused on saying positive things to her. But most of all, I continually told her, 'I love you, and I wish you'd come home.'"

Eventually, Eileen's words made an effect. After a particularly trying showdown with her boyfriend, Trina realized, "I don't have to put up with this. Mom wants me home. And I want to go home." The knowledge of her mom's love gave her the confidence to return to her home.

Life wasn't perfect from then on. But Trina started pulling her life together again. She moved back home to spend a couple of more years with her family and later got an apartment with their blessings. She found a job with a good future. Trina still isn't living the ideal, faith-filled life that Eileen would prefer. But her heart's much closer to her parents, and the Lord, than it has been for years. She's no longer a total stranger to Eileen.

As you know, communicating with the stranger in your house is one of the hardest things imaginable. But our God specializes in grace. And He not only freely shares that grace with us but also enables us to give that grace and love to these children we love so much. We won't always find happy endings in our stories, and our efforts won't always bring the results we crave. But by showing love and support and keeping the lines of communication open, we can once again learn how to build relationships with the strangers in our homes.

For Your Reflection

- Quickly chart what you know about your child's spiritual journey. What kind of faith questions has your child faced that you know about?

- Have you ever felt a need to confront your child's lifestyle? If so, have you done this? If not, what's preventing you?

- Think of a time you've successfully communicated with your child since he or she strayed. Describe the scene in writing. What elements were involved that made the communication so good?

- What are your personal boundaries on communication with your child?

- Read and reflect on Rom. 12. What words of advice can we draw from in this scripture about communicating with our prodigals?

Overcoming
the Overwhelming

6

Beth always had a strong will and a mind of her own, her dad, Rod, admits. But when she started middle school, the trials became worse. Beth left all of her parents' teachings, and rebellion became her sole way of life. Soon, behavior that at its worst resulted in suspension from school quickly turned to more serious behavior as prostitution and drugs.

Rod and Colleen were at the end of their ropes to know how to deal with Beth. "You name it, we probably tried it," Rod wearily recalls. But nothing worked. And Rod and Colleen were left in an eternal abyss of overwhelming emotions.

"When Beth started going so offtrack, I have to say it wasn't as big a shock as it might have been had she always been an angel. But we were still surprised and shocked, hurt and confused. We were angry at God, Beth, society, the justice system, even ourselves," Rod remembers. "I blamed myself for being too soft on Beth, for not seeking help earlier, for avoiding the truth of my child's problems, for being too involved in church, for not being a Christian longer, for not praying enough, for sinning too much after becoming a Christian, for nearly everything you can think of. Some of the thoughts and emotions lasted longer than others."

Besides the stress of trying to figure out why Beth was so

determined to choose the bad side of life, Rod and Colleen tried to figure out what was going on inside their own minds.

When Beth became pregnant and kept taking drugs and living with abusive men, Rod's emotions continued spilling over.

Even if your child hasn't gone to Beth's extremes, you can probably understand the distress Rod and Colleen encountered. These emotional wounds can sap our energy and wear us down. So how can we keep from being totally overwhelmed by the trauma?

Waves of Grief

As Rod illustrates, a prodigal's parent is likely to face all kinds of conflicting emotions: anger, depression, hope, despair, hatred, love, longing to reconcile, wanting detachment. What emotions you feel and when depends on the parent and on the day, or sometimes even the time of day!

Actually, as we've mentioned earlier, when our children go astray, we go through very real loss. We may lose our relationships with them—that child who was always a precious joy has changed. We may have to let go of our dreams of a happy, committed Christian home with all of our children serving God. We may deal with questions and the loss of our own steadfast, secure faith, as we wonder why God doesn't seem to answer our prayers for this beloved child. We may experience a loss of togetherness in our marriages or with our other kids. And we may look at the loss of our dreams for our child's future.

When our child strays, we face grief. We have had a loss. And perhaps it's even a bit more traumatic than a death. A death usually brings closure, but we're less likely to find closure because our child is still living, still building our hopes at times, and often still destroying more of our dreams.

Grief counselor and author Harold Ivan Smith points out

that unlike many people believe, usually grief does not come in stages that we pass through. Rather, grief strikes us in cycles.[15] Grief can be like the waves of the ocean rushing onto the shore. Sometimes the waves of anger may come crashing in: anger at ourselves for not preventing this; anger at the prodigal for acting like an idiot; anger at a spouse; anger at a person who led our child astray; anger at a job that kept us away from home so much; anger at God for not overriding our child's free will.

At other times, we may plunge into a chill of despair or depression leaving us numb, or feel the foam of guilt enveloping us. Part of our grief trail may include humiliation. Heaven knows we parents are always susceptible to feeling like failures when our children do not behave well. The humiliation may be intensified if we're a leader. Added to Rod's despair of his child's straying was the fact that he was a police officer—with a child doing illegal things. Sharon and Matt wondered if they could still be leaders in the church when their son became a prodigal. Jane was running for public office in her community when her daughter became a juvenile delinquent.

Like the ocean waves, sometimes the feelings will crash upon us with more intensity, sometimes we'll just feel gentle waves. Sometimes the tide will be out and we can bask in the sun for a while; sometimes the storm clouds gather and the waves churl and seem to drown us. Many times we'll feel tossed about like a minuscule seashell in the tides.

And like the seashell, we may find our shape being changed. Some of our edges might be made smoother; or we might end up being broken. Just as our prodigals' lives have changed, so have ours.

The fallout of grief varies. Because of the stress of grief, you may worry more than before or become sharp with other people. You might face depression, even to the degree of not want-ing to get up in the morning or not being able to sleep at night. You might feel a need to escape. You might be feeling like you're doing fine with the situation, but then suddenly find yourself plunged back into the emotions. Grief is like tak-ing three steps forward and two steps back. Because we tend to move through it in cycles, you might find even though you thought you were over your anger or another strong emotion that it keeps coming back like a bad dream.

Dealing with the Grief

The main way to deal with the overwhelming feelings we're experiencing when our kids go astray is to remember that these feelings are normal. Because parents are dealing with losses, grief, and eternally mixed emotions, we also need to just cut ourselves some slack. We need to follow some of the same ad-vice we give a person who has faced the death of a loved one.

One of the things you can do is take things easy for a while. Remember you're going through something tough. Yes, some things can be put off and others can't. But try to take it easy. Try to alleviate as much stress as you can. That may mean tak-ing a sabbatical from singing in the choir or teaching Sunday School, or not inviting people over for dinner like you normal-ly do. Some of these activities are good because they remind us that life goes on and give us an interest, or distraction, from the overwhelming feelings. But feel free to just say no to any-thing that will add more negative stress. Don't expect yourself to keep up with your normal pace.

Remember that this experience can affect your body. Dur-ing stressful times we're more likely to experience energy loss, health issues, weight gain or loss, and other uncomfortable physical effects. As if it's not bad enough that our children have become strangers, our very bodies sometimes become strangers to us. When we're going through depressing times, it's easy to ignore our bodies. But in the long run, that exacerbates our problems. We have to take care of ourselves physically by focusing on good nutrition, exercise, and getting enough rest.

Also, treat yourself. Do things that will make you feel better: get a massage, do something unusual that you've been wanting to do, have a special evening with your spouse, go on a family day trip with your other kids.

Never feel guilty for enjoying yourself, even though you may be grieving because of what's going on with your child. Instead, grab the splashes of joy whenever and wherever you can.

Like Rod, many parents find release by journaling their thoughts, no matter how ugly they may seem. On the other hand, some parents hesitate to write their honest thoughts, afraid those words might be seen. If you find relief in expressing yourself on paper or computer, remember you can lock up journals, and computers can lock files with passwords that only you know.

Take Professional Care of Yourself

"Joanna's behavior started to escalate months before she actually left our home and our faith," Karol notes. "While she was still at home, I soon learned that it probably wasn't a matter of *if* we would have a blowup during the evening, but *when*. I'd be thinking everything was fine, and Joanna would suddenly create an unpleasant scene. Eventually, I dreaded going home from work. I was trying my hardest to have a good relationship with this child, but nothing worked. I later realized nothing would work because good relationships take two people, and Joanna enjoyed the scenes."

Before long, Karol felt completely depleted of energy. "During arguments with Joanna, I felt adrenaline surging through me. I was left completely exhausted just by Joanna, forget about my job, family, church, and other responsibilities.

"I started going to the doctor because of my eternal tiredness. He ran tests and found I was a bit iron deficient, but nothing seemed to help. Finally, one day my doctor asked if I could be depressed. I just muttered 'Oh probably.' He encouraged me to try to see if some medication could help. So he described a mild antidepressant.

"I felt a bit stigmatized at first," Karol admits. "Part of me felt like I'd failed spiritually because I couldn't just trust God and snap out of it. But I had also read about brain chemistry and had learned that stress can trigger chemicals that can cause depression, and that medication can be a means God uses to help us get chemicals in our body operating smoothly again."

The medication helped. Karol found it didn't immobilize her mentally or emotionally but took the edge off of the conflicts and mellowed the anger and adrenaline surges. She could finally see some emotional light of day.

"It helped me get some control of myself in the situation," Karol says, "and find the fortitude to say, 'Joanna's moods will not destroy my day or our family.' About six months later, Joanna ran away from home. For almost a year after that, I still took the medication, and it still helped me as I dealt with our daughter. In fact, I could instantly tell anytime I missed a dose; I was edgier. But eventually the stress lessened and I started not noticing if I missed my medication. Not too long after that, I just stopped taking it and have done fine since then. But it was really a lifesaver while I was taking it."

Never hesitate to seek help for yourself when you're going through turmoil. As we've pointed out before, prodigals are usually skilled at knowing just how to press parents' hot spots and often find enjoyment in pushing us to the edge.

When Pauline began facing her own terrible time with Jason, her son, she not only started taking what she called her "happy pills" but for months also spent regular time with a counselor, discussing her challenges with Jason. Some days she survived only by counting the minutes until her next therapy session!

Many parents hesitate to get the professional help they need. Like Karol, we may feel seeking help is a sign of spiritual failure. In a perfect world, maybe it would be. But we live in a fallen world. Yes, we can do all things through Christ who gives us strength (Phil. 4:13), and our God *does* provide all of our needs through His riches in Christ Jesus (v. 19). But sometimes He uses other humans to help us find that strength and to meet our needs. God uses tools, and for you, those tools might include professional help.

Get by with a Little Help from Your Friends

"For the longest time, I kept the burden of our son's lifestyle and attitudes to myself," Kimberly says. "At church, I bit my lips during prayer time to keep from asking for prayer. I was afraid of what people would think. After all, we were leaders in the church."

Finally, Kimberly could stand the silence no longer. She leaked her secret. "Instead of judgment and condemnation, I found instant support," she says. "So many people came up to me in the following weeks and told me that they had been through the experience, that they knew just how I felt, that they were praying for me. The sympathy and encouragement and prayers lightened my burden so much!"

The old adage tells us that sharing our burdens divides our sorrow in half. And that's often true. When you let others know you're dealing with a prodigal child, like Kimberly, you'll be surprised at how many people come out of the woodwork to say, "Been there. Done that. Remember the pain." They provide comfort and prayer support. And they can also provide wisdom when you face a situation you don't know how to handle.

"When I admitted I was dealing with a prodigal I found such help from others," Martha says. "Not only emotionally but also practically. I remember one time when we faced an issue with our son, David, and didn't know what to do. I e-mailed some people I knew had dealt with prodigal kids. Some were very close friends, others were simply people who had expressed sympathy when they learned that we had a prodigal. In my e-mail, I explained our dilemma and asked for advice. Wow! What a wealth of wisdom we got in return! Most had been through a similar experience and could tell us what worked and what didn't work. They brought up points that I'm sure my husband and I never would have thought of otherwise. I'm so glad God brought it to my mind to ask these people for help!"

Maybe you don't like to talk to others about personal details of your life or to share your prayer needs with a room full of people. That's fine. The goal in sharing is to lighten your burden—not to cause more stress by leaving your comfort zone! If you don't feel comfortable letting people know you have a wayward child, don't broadcast it. But do feel free to talk to a close friend or family member who can support you in prayer. Remember, your pastor or small-group leader or Sunday School teacher can be trusted to pray for you, support you emotionally, and keep your confidences.

Letting Go of What We Can't Control

One of the most overwhelming aspects of parenting a prodigal is watching the child make mistakes and do stupid things. We spent many years and so much energy trying to train a child in the way he or she should go spiritually, socially, morally. A prodigal child can remind us of a ball in a pinball machine bouncing from one disaster to another. And we parents are like the paddles in the machine, trying to hit the ball back to the ideal places and away from the pitfalls.

After all, isn't that our job as parents—to direct our kids? To steer them away from the bad and toward the good?

Sure, that's what we try to do from day one. In some ways, the whole first 18 years or so of parenthood is a gradual process of letting go of our kids. We slowly launch them into adulthood and eventually lop off the emotional umbilical cord that has made them somewhat of an appendage of us.

Prodigals, however, tend to speed up that process. They're ready to launch out before we're ready to lop off the cord! We're not ready to let go of all responsibility for our kids yet, understandably, because we see our kids are not ready for the maturity, discipline, and responsibility of adulthood.

"Even after Amber ran away, I still felt like a full-time parent to her," Lin says. "I thought of her constantly. I knew she was sleeping with different guys, experimenting with drugs. I learned she'd quit her job. I felt almost responsible when her phone was cut off because of the huge bills she'd racked up and hadn't paid. After all, her dad and I are very responsible people. I couldn't believe that our daughter was being so irresponsible."

Most of us can understand Lin's perspective. When our kids get offtrack, it's easy for us to focus on them more and more. We long to know what's going on in their lives, but we also dread hearing it! We spend time worrying and praying for them. And we spend a lot of time trying to find ways to subtly or not so subtly give advice, to steer them away from the pitfalls and into the goals of responsible adulthood. It's easy for us to even become obsessed.

"Our Cindi ran away from home with an older man," Stella recalls. "They went to another state and Cindi refused to communicate with us. For the longest time, the only contact I had from her was a post office box in a large city. Nearly every day I'd write her a letter. My whole life focused on hoping I'd hear from her and trying to figure out a way to get her to communicate with us."

When we continually focus on our absent children, we end up living in an up-and-down world—a continual cycle of hope and despair. At some point, we have to decide for our own sanity that enough is enough. We have to realize that life has changed and that our roles have changed in our children's lives.

"The emotional temperature of my days revolved around what was going on with Amber," Lin recalls. "One day one of my coworkers who had also gone through prodigal experiences was straight with me. She pointed out that by leaving home, Amber had placed herself out from under my authority; I could no longer parent Amber the same way I was parenting my other children at home. Amber had ended that stage in our relationship whether I liked it or not and obviously was not going to return to it. So my job as a parent now was to learn a new parenting role. Instead of just knowing how to parent kids I could still control and guide directly, I had to learn how to be a good parent to a kid who was making her own choices—right or wrong."

Realizing that her parenting role was changing also led Lin to make another important decision: She realized she needed to let go of Amber.

"I had to release her to adulthood, allow her to be her own person, wise or unwise," Lin explains. "I had to let go of the notion that anything Amber did was my fault or responsibility. I had to learn that Amber was going to do what she was going to do. Sometimes I'd be able to give her advice, but usually I couldn't. And I had to realize that was OK. I had to detach myself from her actions, from my responsibility for her, from my control of her."

Lin learned to not take on Amber's problems as her own, which included no longer trying to shield Amber from consequences for her own actions. And as Lin released Amber emotionally, she could again focus on her own life. Her days no longer were rated as good or bad depending on what was going on with Amber.

After months of obsessing about Cindi, Stella finally came to the same conclusion; she couldn't spend all of her days worrying about her daughter and writing letters begging her daughter to come home. Stella had a special time of prayer. Realizing that God knew exactly where Cindi was, and that He loved Cindi endlessly, Stella released her daughter into her Heavenly Father's hands. She turned control of Cindi over to the Lord.

Then Stella sat down and wrote another letter to Cindi. This time, the letter didn't scold, plead, or try to manipulate Cindi. Instead, Stella told Cindi that she loved her and was releasing Cindi to herself and to God.

Stella learned to move on with her own life. And when Stella stopped pursuing her daughter and let go of her, Cindi finally started contacting her mom and dad again.

Nothing is more overwhelming than continuing to pretend we are in control of something or someone we lost control of long ago! When we feel overwhelmed as parents of prodigals, perhaps we need to take a serious look at our lives and see if we're trying to hold on to something we should be letting go of. Perhaps we're spending too much time and energy worrying about our child. If our teen is destroying our lives, we need to reevaluate and let go. We need to learn to let go of our old parenting roles and find what roles now lie ahead—friend, adviser, or whatever.

Adjusting to a new way of life and a new way of seeing our parenting responsibilities can be tough. But it's vital for our survival.

Take Care of Yourself Spiritually

"When Carlos walked away from God, I ran to my Bible," Patty says. "I prayed constantly, I pored over the Bible to find promises I could cling to, I spent hours on my knees. The days passed, then the weeks and even months, and instead of coming back to God and us, Carlos moved from bad to worse. I couldn't understand it."

Gradually, Patty started spending less of her day praying and reading her Bible. She'd always been faithful with her devotional time, but now it seemed to wane. "I still went to church, but I didn't seem to get as much out of it," she explains. A once-vibrant faith eventually became weak, and Patty felt like she was just hanging on spiritually by a thread.

Author Wes Tracy describes this common phenomenon as "spiritual fatigue."[16] When we've been raised in our faith to cling to Bible promises and that God will answer our prayers, to so fervently turn to Him and not see His work can wear us out and discourage us.

Even when we're discouraged in our faith, God knows how we feel. After all, we only live through a short time of history and experience the pain of only one or two straying teens. But at any given time in history, God is grieving over millions of prodigals.

God may not answer all of the "why" questions. "Why did my child leave?" But we can take our fears, our questions, our distress, even our anger to God. After all, He knows we're experiencing it anyway. We may not find the answers to all of our theological questions. But as we go to God with them, we will find a concerned Father who grieves with us. We'll find a God who loves our children much more than we ever could. And we'll find a father who is also concerned about us. That's what Rod found.

"God has told me in more ways than one that it is absolute arrogance on my part to think that I can tip God's hand one way or another by my failure," Rod says. "Like when I battled with feeling that God was not answering my prayers for Beth to return to Him because I had failed spiritually and as a father. I have been still, listening hard for God's accusing voice, and all I have heard is Him telling me, 'There, there. It will be all right eventually. Just trust Me.'

"I have felt His hand on my cheek, brushing away the acid tears of regret. His mercy and grace in my heart has let me know that in some ways going down that road of false condemnation is a little like being a prodigal myself. When I was on that road, I was not really listening to Him with grace-healed ears."

Maybe your grief over your child will send you running into the Father's arms. Maybe it will make you distant from your faith. Maybe you'll find yourself somewhere in between. But our relationship with God is that: a relationship. Relationships change, mature, move, fluctuate. Don't let yourself feel guilty that you doubt God, doubt your own spirituality, doubt your faith. Be honest with God about your feelings, your fears, and your failures. If in discouragement or weariness you don't feel like turning to Him, even if your devotional time feels stale or you don't feel that passion spiritually that you once did, still take the time to open His Word, to come before Him.

Rod adds, "Let your readers know that there is still a God out there who weeps with them when they weep and cries for them when they mess up, and holds His breath and says 'Welcome' when they finally believe Him. Check out His answers in His Book. He really is an awesomely good God."

For Your Reflection

- Reflect on a time you've felt overwhelmed as you've faced having a prodigal.
- What losses have you felt?
- Each person's grief takes on its own pattern. What kind of grief pattern have you experienced? What emotions have been prevalent?
- What is the spiritual state of your prodigal? Do you feel any of his or her decisions are a result of intense spiritual warfare?
- How has your experience with your prodigal affected you spiritually? Study Matt. 7:7-11. Write about your love for your child. Next, contemplate and write about the love that you think God has for your child.
- Read Ps. 91. Which scriptures especially seem to speak to you in your situation? Choose one or more scriptures to memorize so the Holy Spirit can minister in your life through them.

Focus on Your Family

7

"What were you even thinking?" Rhonda shouted at her daughter. It was the first time Jessica had ever cheated on a test. She'd been caught and given detention, as well as receiving an F on the test in a subject she couldn't afford a failing grade in.

"Jessie stood there looking at me," Rhonda recalls. "I was just bewildered. She'd always been a hardworking student. I had especially clung to Jessie as being the 'good kid,' I think. It was about three months after her sister had blown off school and run away from home. I remember the thought flashing through my mind: First Kimbra and now Jessie?"

That thought seemed to strike a nerve in Rhonda's brain. With Jessie still staring at her, eyes pools of misery, Rhonda suddenly took on a new, gentler tone, "Jessie, does this have anything to do with Kimbra leaving?"

Jessie started crying. She admitted that she'd been so disturbed about her sister leaving that she'd been unable to concentrate lately. As a result, she didn't feel prepared for her test in history. So she'd spontaneously cheated for the first time. Jessie hiccupped through her tears as she said, "I'm sorry. I know it was so wrong. I'll never do it again."

"I gave her a big hug," Rhonda says. "Then I asked her if she'd like to talk to a counselor about Kimbra leaving. I was so surprised when she said yes. Jessie had always been a person who kept to herself."

Rhonda's husband, Robert, made an appointment for Jessie with their church's family counselor. For Jessie, one session was all it took. Jessie was able to express her problems and get help coping. In her situation, Jessie didn't feel a need to return to the counselor, nor did he feel that she really needed more sessions.

Of course, that may not be the norm. Most people who enter counseling need more than one session to help them cope on an ongoing basis. And all families going through the distress of a prodigal should consider family counseling with or without the prodigal.

Rhonda also contacted Jessie's youth pastor and small-group leader. "I knew these people are in youth ministry because they care about kids," Rhonda says. "I confidentially shared what our family was going through because I thought they may be able to help her in ways I couldn't."

Jessie's needs were a wake-up call for Rhonda. "From then on I kept a closer eye on Jessie," she says a bit sheepishly. "I only wish I had thought sooner about the way her sister's behavior could be affecting her."

Even if a prodigal doesn't leave home, stress still infiltrates the home when a child starts behaving in alarming ways. When one of your children goes astray, all members of the family are affected—not only teens and older elementary children. We parents of prodigals should also be aware that our younger children who can't speak or can't articulate—preschoolers or younger elementary kids—may also feel a loss if a sibling leaves and will also react to stress, even if they don't understand what's going on.

As with Jessie, clues that our children are going through a distressing time might include uncharacteristic misbehavior, sudden quietness, signs of nervousness or fear, bad dreams, depression, lower grades, anger, or any sudden or drastic changes in behavior or attitude.

Focus on the Positive

Like Rhonda, Jolene had a daughter who ended up leaving home. And like Rhonda, Jolene had to be reminded that prodigals affect siblings.

"My friend, Sheena, gave me the wake-up call," Jolene recalls. "I was talking to Sheena about my distress with my daughter. I was so focused on Lindsey that my whole life was affected. Sheena asked, 'How are Susie and Ken doing?' Those are my younger children. I told her I guessed they were OK. But I hadn't really thought that much about them. Sheena set me straight. She pointed out that Lindsey had removed herself from our parenting and was now on her own. But we still had other children at home who needed our love and attention. Sheena reminded me that I couldn't focus so much on Lindsey that the other kids got left out."

When we neglect our kids for the sake of the prodigal sibling, it may also send some wrong messages to them. They may feel we care about the prodigal more than we care about them. Or they may perceive that the way to get our attention is behaving badly. After all, as child behavior specialists tell us, kids figure attention for negative behavior is better than getting no attention at all. He or she may think, "It worked for the prodigal child, so it can work for me!" They may not consciously act out, but they may end up doing so without realizing that's what they're doing, as Jessie did.

We also need to realize that our kids' worlds are shaken a bit. The brother or sister they've always loved and respected is suddenly different. They need extra attention and reassurance from us that we're not going to change, that we're still there for them no matter what another brother or sister does.

If we focus only on the wayward child, our other children may also feel angry and neglected like the prodigal's brother in Luke 15. Fortunately, the brother in this passage expressed his feelings to his father. You may need to address the situation with your children to prevent anger or resentment against you or against the prodigal.

Although we're tempted to think only about the child who's such a worry to us at the moment, as Jolene learned, we simply can't do that. It's difficult, but we parents need to remember to continue to give attention to our other children. While we do this, we need to avoid comparing the "good" child to the prodigal. We can applaud good behavior but should never put the pressure on the remaining children to "not be like your brother" or to make them think we will love them only as long as they behave well.

Protecting Siblings

Besides realizing how her prodigal was affecting Jessie, Rhonda learned another lesson when her daughter found an apartment and wanted Jessie to come over.

"At first it was a no-brainer because Kimbra was living with a guy," Rhonda says. "But a few months later, she was living with another girl. She really wanted Jessie to spend the night with her. When I said no to that, she pressured for Jessie to just spend the evening with her. I hesitated on that. I still didn't feel good about that idea. But I thought maybe I was overreacting and wanting to say no just because Kimbra wanted it so badly. I knew Kimbra really wanted to show off her place to Jessie. And I was so mad at Kimbra that I was afraid maybe I was saying no just to get back at her.

"I was also afraid that Jessie would see Kimbra's situation as glamorous, on her own without having to listen to parents, doing what she wanted to do," Rhonda recalls. "I figured if I let her go, I'd have to have a talk with her about the downsides that Kimbra wasn't about to show her. But on the other hand, even though Jessie was five years younger than Kimbra, I felt Jessie had a better head on her shoulders and was more realistic. Jessie was already disgusted by her sister's behavior and seemed to know better. And after all, Kimbra *was* Jessie's sister, I thought, so maybe I should let her go to Jessie's place."

But as Rhonda analyzed her feelings more, she realized some other elements were affecting her opinions.

"I started thinking about all of the at-risk behavior Kimbra was practicing. Of course, she'd told me she wouldn't do anything bad while Jessie was there. But Kimbra was lying a lot at that time. She had displayed bad judgment so many times that I couldn't really trust her to show good judgment regarding what was appropriate behavior around her sister and what wasn't.

"She was justifying behavior like drinking and smoking and partying and sleeping around. She thought such behavior was cool. Knowing Kimbra's personality, I felt she'd try to impress her sister even if that meant offering her sister a cigarette or bragging about sexual conquests or talking about the glories of drugs. Plus, I had no idea who else would be at the apartment. Maybe Kimbra would plan on no one being there while her sister was there. Then again, Kimbra and her roommate had party reputations, and guys were always showing up with kegs and looking for a good time. What if that happened while Jessie was there? Again, I felt I couldn't trust Kimbra to show good judgment and protect her sister from such influences.

"I realized I didn't trust Kimbra at that stage of her life, and I couldn't take a chance with something happening to Jessie.

Even if it made Kimbra mad at me for a long time, I couldn't put Jessie at risk for the sake of peace or a relationship with Kimbra."

Talking to the Kids

What do you say to the kids at home when a brother or sister has become a prodigal? We can't just ignore the situation and pretend our kids won't notice the problems or the stress.

"We were honest with Jessie," Rhonda says. "She knew her sister left. So we explained that what Kimbra was doing was wrong. We didn't try to sugarcoat it for Jessie or make any excuses for Kimbra. At the same time, we emphasized that we as a family needed to pray for Kimbra. We did take time to pray about Kimbra with Jessie.

What you say may also depend on the age of the other children at home. You may also have to consider what you will and won't say about the prodigal in front of the other children.

Since Jessie was a teenager and was facing her own choices, Rhonda explains that she and Robert would sometimes discuss aspects of dealing with a prodigal in front of Jessie. Like when Kimbra faced various difficulties. "I wanted Jessie to know what kinds of problems kids faced when they ran away from home and ran away from God," Rhonda says. "At times we made sure we talked behind closed doors, but most of the time we let Jessie in on it. Of course, as a result of that, Jessie had a lot of questions, and I had to go ahead and explain things. For instance, Kimbra told Jessie that she was sexually active. So Robert and I didn't hesitate to discuss the dangers of Kimbra's promiscuity in front of Jessie. As a result, I had to be prepared to talk to Jessie about STDs."

On the other hand, Jolene was guarded about what she discussed in front of her children because they were much younger. When the children talked about Lindsey not living with them anymore, Jolene simply told them, "Let's pray that she'll come home quickly." She felt it was not appropriate or wise to discuss any of Lindsey's inappropriate behavior in front of the children.

Sometimes we're fortunate and have a child like Jessie who understands that her sister is wrong and tends to feel a sympathy and bond with her parents over the situation. But that's not always the case. Sometimes younger children don't understand. They may become angry with us, especially when we curtail their time spent with the prodigal or set boundaries for the prodigal that appear cruel. It can be a double whammy having a prodigal and having our other children angry with us. Explaining the situation and praying that God will help the younger child understand is sometimes the best parents can do.

We also need to watch the attitude of the children at home toward the prodigal. Kids don't like to see their parents in pain. A child may be angry with the brother or sister who causes so much pain in the family.

After letting the child express the anger, we can encourage the child to spend that energy trying to love the brother or sister and praying for him or her, asking God to help him or her love and minister to that sibling.

Till Prodigal Do Us Part

Our relationships with our children aren't the only bonds we need to protect when confronting the issues of prodigal kids. Marriages can also suffer.

"I realized much more quickly than Harold when Ally began to stray," Ellen says. "He thought I was crazy when I began to mention Ally's behavior and what I felt might be going on. When I told him I thought Ally was drinking, he said I was imagining things. He accused me of being suspicious and dramatic and was even angry with me for thinking such things.

"As I became more certain that Ally was involved in some bad things, Harold was still denying it and we started having some pretty bad fights. By the time Harold learned that I was right, our marriage was encrusted with bitterness. Harold almost acted like it was my fault as if my noticing Ally's behavior caused it. We were pretty angry with each other for quite some time."

As in Harold and Ellen's case, when one parent suspects the prodigal's wayward wanderings and the other doesn't, the marriage ties can become tested or even knotted. The parent denying the problem may feel a shock that the other can be disloyal to the child. His or her refusal to believe the other parent can lead to a lack of trust and deep hurt. Prodigals sometimes exacerbate the problem by pitting one parent against the other.

Marriages also face serious division with another common problem: the blame game. As we've discussed before, when a child goes astray, we often want to find a reason for the child's behavior, thinking if we can find the reason, we can fix it.

Accordingly, in our distress, frustration, and pain, it's especially hard for us not to point fingers.

"If you hadn't spoiled him . . ." "You should have been more aware of where he was and what he was doing . . ." "I told you we shouldn't let her hang out with that girl, but you said it was OK . . ."

Such words only send parents into opposite corners. And whether or not they're true, the accused always walks away feeling guilty. In accusing a spouse, we're piling the pain higher on the person we're supposed to love the most on earth. The accuser may think, "Oh, he knows I'm only venting, that I don't really mean it." But we can't count on that. It's still cruel to do—and wrong.

When our kids go astray, we have to remind each other that this was the *child's* choice. It wasn't anything we did or didn't do or that our spouse did or didn't do. Our child is old enough to walk down a righteous or unrighteous path.

Andrew and Diana both bemoaned the fate of their son, but the two didn't end up in opposite emotional corners until they disagreed on whether or not to bail out their son, Mark, financially. Mark had racked up many bills and was being sued by one of his creditors. He asked his parents for money to pay off the debt. Andrew wanted to loan Mark the money. Diana felt they should withhold the money and let Mark face whatever consequences came from his lack of financial responsibility. She felt if they loaned Mark the money, he'd never repay it.

Many times couples disagree on how to respond to their prodigal child. Often, one holds more of a justice standpoint, while the other wants to show mercy. Like Andrew and Diana, both end up in opposite corners, glaring at each other like a couple of boxers on the sidelines.

Holding It Together

Anytime we have a prodigal child, we need to be prepared for the challenges it causes in our marriage. Instead of letting the problems tear apart the fabric of our marriage, we need to be sensitive to remain in one piece. Spouses need to realize that they're a team—allies. Both love the child and want the same objective: for the child to return to the fold. Both parents are distressed and hurting and deep down both parents are feeling like failures.

It's easy to suffer our own pain and to not be aware of, ignore, or diminish our partner's pain. But perhaps one of the best things we can do is to remember that our spouse is in pain, like a wounded soldier on the edge of the parenting battlefield. How would we treat a wounded person? Sensitively. We certainly wouldn't want to inflict more pain. Instead, we'd want to bring healing.

One couple who has been married for 20 years said their secret to a happy marriage is to "Just be nice. We're supposed to be a haven for each other so we just try to be nice," the husband explains. The same advice can hold true for spouses who are parents of prodigals. A little kindness and sensitivity can go a long way. As well as protecting our relationship, we can protect each other.

In the practical realm of dealing with a straying teen, spouses can work hard to respect and truly listen to each other's opinions.

"Mike and I were always disagreeing on how to deal with Cynthia," Carolyn recalls. "It got so I just stopped even listening to his opinions, and honestly, didn't think very much of him because I thought he was too soft. But then one day, when we disagreed yet again, I dug a little deeper and asked Mike questions about why he felt we should handle the situation a certain way. I realized that Mike had the same final goal that I did, even though his opinion on how to get there was different from mine. I realized his idea made sense. So I stepped back, let him handle it, and was surprised when his idea did work."

It's important for us to continue to listen to each other and to respect each other's opinions, even when we don't agree. Again, sometimes we need to remind ourselves that we both have the same desire and goal in mind, finding the best way to reach the child. When facing a decision regarding the child, it's important to seek our spouse's input instead of just moving ahead. When spouses discuss options and actions together, rather than acting independently, it reaffirms the "team" feeling.

Sometimes we will disagree, as Carolyn and Mike did. At

those times, we will either have to find a compromise or one spouse will have to give in. When we're the one giving in, it's best to do so graciously. And if the spouse's idea doesn't work, as we predicted, we need to just keep our mouths shut instead of pronouncing an "I told you so." The other spouse realizes when a plan has failed. We can just graciously sympathize and move ahead.

Even when couples agree on how to treat prodigals, and when blame and other matters aren't an issue, they still need to safeguard their marriage. Chuck and Andrea were both distressed about their child. They found themselves spending hours contemplating what to do about various situations and problems of their prodigal. They worried together and out loud. Soon, too many of their conversations revolved around their prodigal, and their marriage ended up being affected. They no longer knew how to talk together about anything else except their child and the problems.

When this happens, it's time to set some boundaries.

Our marriage relationships need to come first. After all, God intended for spouses to be together for a whole lifetime—long after the kids have moved away and long after the kids have gone through their prodigal stages. At times, we just have to set boundaries regarding how far we will allow a prodigal to emotionally impede our relationship. We have to just say no to sitting around discussing our prodigal for hours. Or we may need to put boundaries on when we discuss the prodigal; such as, never at bedtime. We have to move ahead with our own lives and marriages, making time for ourselves and our relationship with each other. In the long run, keeping a strong marriage is best for us and for our kids who are still at home—and, in turn, for our prodigals too.

Protecting Other Family Members

Extended family is affected by a prodigal. Rhonda invited her sister's family to join them for dinner. She debated whether or not to invite Kimbra. After all, she was always looking for ways to minister to Kimbra and build the family bond. On the other hand, Rhonda thought of her young nieces, one Jessie's age and one younger.

Although Kimbra had promised Rhonda she'd never talk about inappropriate things with Jessie, Rhonda knew Kimbra had bragged about her sexual conquests to Jessie. "I had to face the fact that Kimbra would probably also brag about her behavior to my nieces," Rhonda says. "I felt like I had no right to expose my nieces to that, and I didn't want to put my sister and her husband in a predicament of having to deal with it. I felt I needed to protect my nieces.

"After all, I wouldn't have wanted anyone else to subject my daughter to that kind of situation and I realized I couldn't take the chance. Our families got together without Kimbra and while the kids were playing elsewhere, I explained to my sister what had happened regarding Kimbra. I was glad I did. She has faithfully supported me since then."

When Charlene's son moved out of the house and in with some older friends, he had soon gone through his money and was asking Charlene for a loan. Charlene refused. Her son, Blaine, was furious and said he'd find the money somehow. Charlene immediately thought of her parents and picked up the phone.

"I told them that Blaine had moved out," she said. "I warned them that he was involved with some rough characters and that I was afraid he was doing drugs. I felt my parents needed to know in case Blaine went to them for money or took his friends to their house. I was a bit concerned for their safety. I didn't think Blaine would ever hurt them, but then again, people do unexpected things if they're on drugs. I didn't know what my son's friends might do to his grandparents if they were desperate and saw them as an easy target. I've read too many stories of stuff like that happening!"

Like most elderly people, Charlene's parents understood and promised not only to be alert but also to support Charlene's stance to let Blaine face his own consequences. They honored her request when she asked them not to bail him out financially. Although Blaine was the first child in the family to be a prodigal, Charlene's parents had seen the same thing happen in many of their friends' families, and promised to pray for Blaine and for Charlene. And thanks to Charlene's filling them in on the situation, her parents were also prepared to love and talk to Blaine in a way that he wouldn't accept from Charlene at the time.

The old adage tells us that no person is an island. That's especially true when a prodigal is in our family. Our child's actions affect every family relationship. So when your child strays, be prepared to explain the situation to others and protect others who may also be affected. Remember that no matter how emotionally cold it may seem at times, our other relationships shouldn't be sacrificed for the sake of a child who, frankly, probably won't be helped until he or she decides to change.

The benefit of letting others know that your child is going through a tough, wayward time is that more people are praying for, loving, and supporting your entire family unit.

For Your Reflection

- What have your other children thought about your straying teen's current lifestyle?

- How much time have you spent focusing on your rebellious child? On your other children? How can you give more attention and focus to the kids still at home?

- What percent of your conversations with your spouse revolve around your prodigal? How much of your conversation *should* focus on this child? If you need to reduce the amount of time spent focusing on this child, how can you do so?

- What specific actions can you take to build your marriage at this time?

- How can you support your spouse right now and bring refreshment and encouragement to his or her soul?

- Read Ps. 68:1-19. Does the thought of protecting others make you feel as if you're carrying a heavy burden? Commit this to the Lord. Reflect on verse 19 and list ways He has taken your burden. You might want to memorize this and Matt. 11:28-30.

Is Coming Home Really an Option?   8

"Mom, I want to come home."

When Joan heard her son's voice on the phone, her heart melted. For days, even months, she had prayed fervently to hear those words. She wanted to shout. Instead, she took a deep breath and calmly said, "Why don't you come over and let's talk about it."

She mentally calculated how long it would take Randy to walk home from his friend's house, where he'd been living for four months. She tried not to get too excited as she forced herself to keep away from the window. Of course, she wanted to just stand there waiting for him. She wanted to run out through the neighborhood like the prodigal father in the Bible—arms wide open, shouting, and inviting everyone to a party.

Instead, she restrained herself. It wasn't just that she didn't want her neighbors to see her looking like a demented fool scampering on the streets. She knew before she welcomed Randy back home that the time had to be right—that Randy had to be ready to come back home.

Joan kept busy cleaning in the kitchen until she heard the tentative knock on the front door.

"I opened the door and looked at my son's face, and I knew. I knew the horrible time was over," Joan says, her voice dropping to a whisper and tears edging her blue-gray eyes.

"My son had left arrogant and determined, thinking that drugs and partying were all that was important in life, hating me because I made him choose between his drugs and his home. Now he stood there. He had one of those expressions he'd always had when he was a little boy and had admitted doing wrong; a look like he felt badly for what he'd done and was hoping I'd love him anyway."

Joan put aside her calm, "we'll see" demeanor. She opened her arms wide and grabbed her son as the tears exploded.

"In the following days I watched him and we talked a lot," Joan says. "And I found my first impression from those moments at the door were right. Randy had changed. He'd dropped the marijuana and dropped those friends. He'd had enough and had no desire to go back."

Fairy Tales and Frustrations

When children leave, many parents experience the same fairy tale ending that Joan did. The child is home and life is happy ever after. But that's not always the case.

Pam and Jack were delighted when their daughter Samantha came home. But their joy was short-lived.

"Samantha was back home, but that was about it," Pam says. "She'd stormed out in anger a couple of months earlier because she didn't want anyone telling her what to do. And she was still exactly the same kid who'd left."

"We realized things had changed in those two months," Jack explains. "We realized that Samantha had moved out because she felt she wasn't receiving the privileges an 18-year-old should have. So when she moved back in, Pam and I determined to loosen the rules, to give Samantha the benefit of the doubt and to give her more of that freedom she craved, even if we didn't feel like she was ready for it. But she was still in high school, so for Samantha's good, we didn't feel like we could throw all rules to the wind."

"About the only rule we held on to was for bedtime on a school night," Pam picks up. "We told her we felt she should be in bed by midnight. Samantha was not a good student, and we'd found that she needed her sleep to pass her classes. But the first night home, she went out with a friend and stayed out until 3 A.M. Considering the kind of people she'd been hanging around, we were worried sick."

The next day, Pam and Jack talked to Samantha about following rules.

"But that was just like waving a red flag," Jack says. "Within two days, our whole family was in turmoil again, just as we'd been before Samantha moved out."

"It's like she was purposely pushing everyone's buttons," Pam says. "Like she wanted us all mad for some reason."

When the melee died down a bit, Jack called the whole family to the dining room table to talk.

"We tried really hard not to make it a 'The rest of our family vs. Sam' thing," Jack says. "I told her that we loved her and wanted her home. But I also told her we had to all live together in peace. She just sat and stared straight ahead the whole time with a hateful look I'd never seen before."

"Jack was really gentle," Pam recalls. "He shared some scripture with Sam and talked to her about behavior. He told her that we had cut back on the parenting rules, but that living together meant being considerate of others. I don't think any dad could have done better in such circumstances."

"Once in a while a tear would trickle out," Jack said. "But there was no other response. I was upset the next morning when we woke up and Sam was gone, but I wasn't really surprised."

Why can't it always work out for a prodigal child to return

home? Perhaps part of the reason concerns the motive behind the child wanting to return.

Perhaps the prodigal father in the Bible could welcome his son so readily and instantly because he could immediately tell, like Joan, that his son was repentant and was coming home with the right motives.

But often our prodigals return with the wrong motives.

"I think the main reason Sam wanted to return home was because she was broke, her boyfriend kicked her out, and she didn't have anyplace else to go," Pam says. "She wasn't necessarily ready to come home. It was just the easiest option."

When a child wants to come back home, for most parents, it may be best to follow Joan's example: instead of immediately throwing open the door and killing the fatted calf, say, "Come on around and let's talk about it."

"I wish we'd done that before Sam came home," Pam says. "It would have helped us realize we'd be walking back into the same nightmare we'd had when Sam was at home and rebellious. Perhaps talking with Sam about why she wanted to come home would have helped her see that maybe coming home wasn't what she really wanted. She wasn't ready to put herself under our authority or to live with others in peace. It might have been easier on all of us."

Focusing on the Family . . . Again

Besides analyzing a child's reasons for wanting to come home, we should also evaluate some other factors. In the last chapter, we discussed the effects that wayward kids can have on the rest of the family.

When Elizabeth's prodigal wanted to move back home, Elizabeth felt the situation would be too detrimental for her other children.

"Our daughter was out of high school," Elizabeth explains. "She'd dropped out of college, and I was pretty certain she wanted to come home not because she'd changed her ways and wanted to be with us but because it would be a lot less expensive to live with us."

Elizabeth felt her daughter still showed too many signs of bad behavior, irresponsibility, partying, and drug use. So Elizabeth and Jonathan refused to let her come home. Elizabeth feared her daughter not only might come home high or drunk but also might bring friends she didn't want around her other children.

Jordan faced the same decision when his daughter, Katie, wanted to come home. Jordan let Katie come home knowing she was still living the wild life. He made strict rules about Katie's behavior in the home. But despite his precautions, Katie's younger brother was still affected. Within months he was sneaking out of the house to join Katie at parties. The 15-year-old boy lost his virginity to one of Katie's friends, and over the next several years, traveled down the same road as Katie.

"I wish I'd trusted my instincts more and my daughter less," Jordan now explains. "I wanted to help my daughter, and I'd hoped to reach her, but now I feel I sacrificed my son in the process of trying to help a girl who really didn't want help or wasn't ready for it."

Your prodigal may not try to lead your other kids into sin, but how will they treat the other kids? Will they be kind and good for them, or will they be mean to them? What kind of treatment will your children have to put up with if the prodigal returns?

On the other side of the coin, how do other children in your home feel about your prodigal returning home? If the children express hesitancy, fear, or reluctance at the thought, probe into their feelings. Think about their perspectives when you consider letting a child come home.

Making It Work

In the blessed event when a child truly is ready to come home, how can we parents help increase the odds that the situation will work out?

The first step might be to figure ahead of time what the rules need to be. What kinds of things will you put up with or not put up with from your prodigal?

About eight months after she'd first moved home and then out again, Samantha wanted to come back home yet again. During those months Samantha was gone, Pam and Jack thought through what the conditions should be if Samantha ever truly wanted to come back home.

"By that time, Samantha was out of high school and had been paying for an apartment with her friend. Our home already had an apartment on the lower level, so we told Sam she could rent out our lower level," Pam explains.

The couple decided it would work best to give Samantha the same rules they'd give any other boarder: no boyfriends overnight, no smoking or drinking, treating the furniture well, and notice if she was going to have late-night, loud parties. Samantha would provide her own food and cook in her own apartment. Pam and Jack decided they didn't want Sam doing cosmetic revisions on their basement until they were sure the situation would work out.

After we set rules, boundaries, or guidelines for our prodigals, the next step is to clearly communicate those directives and expectations.

To make sure the boundaries were firmly drawn, Pam and Jack created a contract. The paper included their rules, the amount Samantha would pay, when she would pay it, and what responsibilities were hers and what responsibilities were theirs. The contract even included specifics on such things as laundry room usage and yard usage. Sam had free use of the family deck, provided that she'd notify them if she wanted to use the deck or yard for a party. In turn, they promised privacy for her. They specified that Samantha would knock on the door before bursting into their home, and that they would also knock before entering Sam's apartment. They noted what the terms would be for ending the rental situation.

"We put in the contract everything we thought could even be an issue," Jack recalls.

Sam, Jack, and Pam sat down together and talked through the contract to make sure everyone understood the expectations of both parties. Then all three signed the contract.

Jack and Pam also emphasized to Sam that they felt the contract should be followed on a trial basis. They would all reevaluate the contract after three months to make sure the situation was working.

You may not want to set up a contract or charge rent for your prodigal, especially if the child is still in high school. However, if he or she is working, it's good to help him or her gain responsibility by making a rental payment. If you really feel your child is struggling financially, it can be a small payment. Even if you don't have an apartment in your basement, in a world where kids in their 20s are returning home to live with Mom and Dad, you may still want to ask your child to make a payment to help with groceries and rent.

Before you let a prodigal child come home, do set up guidelines. Spell out what you expect from the prodigal. Even if you don't have a contract, it's good to write out your expectations or "Guidelines for our household" for your returning child. Asking him or her to sign the sheet will give the step more validity. You may even include all family members in the house. If you do set a contract for your child, you may want a witness, such as a counselor or other objective party, to also be present and sign.

Most importantly, before you let the child return, determine what you will do if he or she does not live up to the expectations. Decide the consequences beforehand, then communicate those to your child ahead of time. Make sure they're consequences you can live with. For instance, if you tell a child she will be kicked out immediately if she smokes in your home, you need to be prepared to do that instead of letting her stay in your home until she finds another place to live. So think about outcomes very carefully. And if your child crosses the boundary, follow through immediately.

That's tough for a parent to do, especially since prodigals tend to be strong-willed children who *will* test the limits. Remember that nothing is wrong with setting boundaries. You're not showing less love for your child by doing this, but are helping your child. By doing so, you are not enabling the child to continue in self-destructive behavior.

Why Am I Letting My Child Come Home?

In the process of deciding whether or not to let a prodigal return home, you also have to take a look into your own heart.

Earlier we mentioned determining our prodigals' motivations, but sometimes we need to determine our own motivations. Why do we want the prodigal back home so badly instead of letting him or her live his or her own life? Do we want our children to come back home because we can't stand to cut the apron strings? Do we want the wayward child back home to prove to ourselves that we're not failures? Is it a matter of pride?

If we're honest with ourselves and find one of those reasons to be the motivation, then we want our child home with the wrong motive—we want the child home for *us.* And chances are, the situation won't work out.

Other motives can also be tricky. Do we want the child back home so we can control his or her life? This can be a good motive if the child is still underage and needs to have parental authority. But if one reason a child strayed in the first place stems from a control issue, expect difficulties if you're still trying to maintain the same level of control.

Other parents, like Rod and Colleen, let their children come back home hoping to help save the child from himself or herself. Unfortunately, as Rod and Colleen learned, sometimes this doesn't work out because the child doesn't want to be saved. No matter how badly we want to, we simply can't help a prodigal, no matter how hard we try, until he or she wants to be helped.

Who Am I Now?

Another step to take in your own life before you let a child return home is to analyze what your role will now be. Joan and Randy were able to return to their old situation with Joan as the parent and Randy as the child under her authority, as if Randy had never left. That may be the case for you, too, especially if your child is younger or still in school. But more times than not, parents will have to reevaluate their roles.

"When Samantha decided to come home again, I realized we had to move into a new relationship," Pam mentions. "I realized that my daughter had been living on her own and had taken herself outside of the realm of my authority. I had to realize that Sam was now her own person, her own adult. She was no longer a child under my authority. As my daughter, she was, and always will be to some degree, influenced by me. But I could no longer treat her as an underage child. I had to start accepting her as an adult and move into the role of 'mom of a grown-up kid.' I had to move to more of a friend role."

For Pam, this was a new step, since Samantha is her oldest child. For some parents, especially those who already have older children away from home, this might be an easier step. But if it's time for us to move to this new role with this child, the time to face that realization is before the child comes home.

We can even communicate to our returning prodigals, "Look, you've clearly expressed to me that you're an adult now, so I'm treating you like an adult. That works both ways. I will always be your parent, but I will no longer direct you or 'parent' you as if you were a younger child and still my responsibility. I will give you advice when you ask for it or when I feel it's appropriate, but I realize you can choose whether or not to follow it, or even to listen. And on the other hand, I expect you to act like an adult, to be responsible, so I won't be tempted to step back into a more involved parenting role. We both need to realize that our relationship is adjusting now to your new status in life."

By communicating this to your prodigal, you're also fostering an atmosphere of understanding that gives you more freedom to learn together. It will be easier to apologize when you step over your own boundaries and to communicate as both you and your prodigal adapt to the new relationship. For instance, you'll feel more freedom to say, "Carol, I'm sorry I ordered you to be back home by midnight last night. I realize the hours you keep are your own business."

And you can more freely address the real issue, "But my real problem is that when you come home so late, it wakes up your little brother and he has a hard time falling asleep. Can you help me think of a way to solve this problem?" or "Carol, I realize you're not a kid and don't have a curfew anymore. But while you're living at home, I can't help worry about you if you're out past midnight. If you realize you're going to be out really late, would you call me just as a courtesy so I'll know you're OK and not out lying in a ditch somewhere?" After a child has left home, anytime he or she returns, the dynamics in the home have changed. It's inevitable, and we must realize that before we can move ahead.

What's the Worst That Could Happen?

As much as we hope and pray for the best, when we're looking at the idea of a prodigal returning home, we also have to consider what the worst-case scenario might be. For instance, the thought did cross Rod's mind that his daughter's return home might lead to his son being swayed the wrong way. However, he dismissed the thought as negative, so he wasn't prepared to deal with the worst when it did happen.

What are potential problems that could happen if your child moves back home, and are you prepared to deal with them? If not, don't let your child come home yet.

Also, in looking at factors concerning letting your child come home, consider your feelings about the matter.

To all outward signs, William was ready to come back home. He was sorry he'd stomped away. He felt he'd learned his lessons. He was even willing to follow Martha's rules. But Martha still had a dread in her heart. She still had a fear it wouldn't work out.

"I just had a bad feeling about it, one I couldn't explain," she says. "It wasn't logical, but it was there, and though I never would have admitted to myself or anyone else, I didn't really want him to come home. I just wasn't ready. I'd had such battles with William that I was just plain tired. I felt wounded. And I didn't feel strong enough yet to even want to begin to deal with William. I loved my son, but even though I tried, I couldn't make myself be excited about the thought of his coming home. I secretly dreaded it."

So evaluate whether or not *you* are ready for your child to return. If you aren't, you aren't. Don't feel guilty, and don't feel like you're "unspiritual" or a bad parent or a horrible person if you're not ready to take the risk yet. Be honest with yourself and with your spouse. And you don't have to go into details with your child. You can simply say, "I don't think that will work out right now, but let's look at the possibility again in two months."

Coming Home

Just as Pam and Jack set up a contract on a trial basis, you may want to let your child come home on trial to see how it works out for both of you. After all, your son or daughter may think he or she can live within your guidelines but may find out once home that it won't work after all. Designating a trial basis up front can give you and your child the freedom to be honest with each other. Make sure you communicate to your prodigal that it's a trial for both of you, not just to see if he or she can live up to your expectations. Right up front determine that all parties involved will sit down together at the end of this trial period and evaluate the arrangement. In fact, you might want to have one of these evaluation times a couple of weeks after the prodigal first comes home.

If the situation is not working, talk with your child. See if you can all come up with a creative solution together. Or perhaps your child will want you to change something. If the child is asking you to make a change that you just can't do (perhaps Carol wants you to stop expecting her to call you if she'll be in after midnight, but you just can't promise that you can let go of that expectation), be honest. If you want to try to make the change, let your child know you'll try, but don't make promises you can't keep. Your child needs to trust you as much as you need to feel you can trust him or her.

If you have a problem that can't be resolved, don't feel "guilted" into letting the child remain at home.

Sally had prayed for months that her son Clint, an alcoholic, would return home. He finally did. Clint returned home with the proper attitude, and he really wanted to make it work. But Clint and his dad, Bob, had always had personality conflicts. And no matter how hard both tried, they constantly ended up battling.

Sally was soon an absolute wreck. The constant tension between Clint and Bob affected her nerves and was wearing her down. She was heartbroken, and she was also torn—both of these men she loved so much unconsciously put pressure on her to side with them. And though Sally could see both of their perspectives, nothing she did helped them get along.

Finally, Sally and Bob had to ask Clint to leave. Clint was sincerely trying to pull his life back together and was doing as well as a recovering alcoholic can do. But in the process, Clint really couldn't afford his own place. So considering the tensions between the men, Bob and Sally felt the best way they could help their son was not to let him live at home but to help him pay his rent.

"It was hard on us because we didn't make too much money," Sally recalls. "But it ended up being the best decision we could have made. Clint felt supported and still visited us often. He and Bob loved spending time together, they just couldn't live together. It was well worth our sacrifice. And soon Clint was on his feet and didn't need our help anymore."

You Don't Have to Be a Bible Hero

"My son was lost, but now he's found!" the father of the prodigal proclaimed in the much-beloved Bible story. He was so excited about his son's return that he even threw a huge bash, inviting everyone to celebrate with him that his son had come home.

But this story that brings us so much hope also brings us so much needless guilt! Because the prodigal father was so excited about his son, we feel we should automatically let a child come back home. But we forget a couple of things:

- This was just a story, an illustration. Jesus told this to help us understand God's fatherly love for us. It was to encourage us when we're wayward to return to the Father. And it shows us the Father's response to His children who have strayed. This can be a wonderful, powerful example for many of us to follow when our children do go astray. But it's not necessarily a guideline for us to follow with our prodigals.

- Even if we took the prodigal story as an example to concretely follow, we have to realize that in the story everything was lined up in good shape. The son came home after wallowing among the pigs, repentant enough that he was just looking to serve his father for room and board —he was just looking for a good employer. He had learned his lesson.

As we've discussed in this chapter, our kids who want to come home may not have that same wonderfully thankful attitude that the son displayed. If our kids walk in the door snarling at us, we wouldn't be too wise to order the fatted calf killed or to celebrate too soon!

Just because the prodigal's father welcomed his son back doesn't mean we should always instantly roll out the red carpet.

It's a hard trial for a parent's soul, but we have to pray for wisdom and discernment instead of just acting on our feelings. If we act prematurely, we hurt not only ourselves but also our prodigal and any others in the situation.

Often, the time is never right for a child to come back home; loving from a distance is the necessary answer. As we follow God's guidance, when the time and situation is right, most of us eventually get to welcome a prodigal home—emotionally if not physically!

For Your Reflection

- If you have a prodigal who left home and has now returned, reflect on the situation. Did you instantly let the child return or did you consider some of the things we've mentioned in this chapter?

- What do you wish you had done differently? What do you wish you had thought about earlier?

- If you have a prodigal still out wallowing in the pigpens, what would you do if the prodigal wanted to return home today? Under what conditions would you allow that to happen? What boundaries would you set?

- How do, or would, your spouse and children feel about the prodigal returning home?

- Reflect on the word and idea of "repentance." How important is it to you that your child repents or turns from his or her behavior before he or she comes home?

- Read the prodigal story in Luke 10:15-32. Ask the Lord to show you how this scripture applies to your life. Reflect on how the characters in your life are similar to or different from those in this scripture. How can it bring you hope and healing—not guilt?

Dealing with the Tough Stuff

9

Some kids walk away from the Lord and their families, some kids *run!*

Two of George's three children were sprinters. "Our second child, Shannon, was always strong-willed," George recalls. "During junior high she ran away from home. The police brought her back. After some time, she ran again."

Shannon did about everything involved in a parent's worst nightmare. She sneaked out of the windows at night, got involved in prostitution, dated a thief, became pregnant, did drugs, repeatedly assaulted her mother and little sister, had her child taken away from her by Social Services, aborted another child—you name it. If it was detrimental, Shannon tried it.

After some time, she got her older brother, Tom, involved with her lifestyle. Soon he was "living la vida loca": doing drugs, getting his girlfriend pregnant, stealing, leaving home. He ended up in and out of juvenile detention centers. Finally, Tom asked his parents if he could come home.

"We agreed and set up rules," George says. "Conditions on his returning home, nothing too draconian. But he blew it and brought about 12 ounces of speed into our house."

Then George had to face one of the toughest decisions a parent could ever have to make. "I had to call the police when I discovered it and, of course, Tom was arrested again. This time he didn't return to our house."

What to do when a child is taking part in illegal activity is a difficult decision to make. Like most issues involving prodigals, no set answers exist. Why not just turn a blind eye to the whole thing and hope your child comes to his or her senses?

Some considerations to make if your child is participating in illegal activities:

1. When a child does something, like hosting a keg party for underage guests or bringing illegal substances into your home, you may be held accountable. Many states are considering and passing legislation that makes parents responsible when kids misbehave. Time in jail and fines are being granted to parents who can't control their kids—knowingly, or even unknowingly.

2. Besides opening ourselves up to government censure, if our kids participate in certain activities in our homes and someone gets hurt, we may face lawsuits. For instance, what if your son has a friend over, they snort some coke in his bedroom, and the friend ends up becoming ill or doing something drastic like jumping out a window or hurting himself while climbing on the roof? You're not immune from being held accountable for letting this activity occur in your home.

3. What is best in the long run for your child? "We called the police on Bill when he was bringing drugs into our home," Abby explains. "Nothing was waking Bill up to how he was destroying his life. Of course, we didn't do it vindictively, although at times we were angry enough with Bill! We'd warned him that we would do this, and so we did. And we supported him through the legal processes he had to go through as a result. In our case, that end-

ed up being the catalyst that helped Bill see he didn't really want to continue in the lifestyle he was choosing. Yes, it was hard for quite a while and Bill wouldn't speak to us for months. But 10 years later, he admitted that our taking that step turned his life around."

4. How is your child's behavior affecting other people? If a parent knows his child is a drug dealer, yet does nothing legally about stopping his child from dealing, is that parent partially responsible morally for what happens to the people his child has dealt to? No, we can't be held responsible for our children's sins, but will God hold us accountable if we know our child is destroying others and we don't do anything about it?

Anytime we report a child, it's likely to cause our child to be alienated from us. Our kids may accuse us of being heartless or of not loving them. Actually, striving to help them get to a place where they'll put an end to their downward spiral is the most loving thing we can do.

When Our Prodigal Is Addicted

What if a child is doing drugs? For some reason, prodigals and drugs seem to go hand in hand, even if our kids aren't bringing home 12 ounces of speed, as George's son was.

If you know where your child is getting the drugs, report it. Elaine's daughter was just starting on her downward spiral when Elaine learned she had been smoking marijuana at a friend's house. Elaine was especially furious when she learned the friend's mom had supplied the drug as well as alcohol.

"Our city has an anonymous 'tips hotline' and I called that," she explains. "I had to give them her name and address. I don't know if anything ever came of it, but I feel I did my duty. I could have confronted the mother, but I figured if this woman didn't have qualms about her behavior, my complaints weren't going to change her. And if I had complained to her as well as contacting the police, I was afraid there might be some backlash—that my family or my daughter might end up in danger."

The Focus on the Family Physicians counsel recommends that parents find out just how much the problem has progressed. They recommend that we not only talk to the drug-abusing child but also talk to other family members, the child's friends, and anyone else who can give us insight.[17]

Often a drug user is unwilling to admit that he or she has an addiction. At that point, you and your family may need to confront your child with a pastor or counselor. The confrontation should include options for treatment, such as Narcotics Anonymous or Alcoholics Anonymous, a drug treatment program, a halfway house, or one of the other drug treatment programs available.

If the child is living in your home, you might need to ask him or her to leave if he or she refuses to take steps to overcome the problem. Here again, you might need to practice some especially tough love. You'll need to have patience and courage. Drug addictions and situations usually aren't settled overnight.

If your child is addicted to drugs, expect him or her to show "addict logic." This is a mind-set that rationalizes any action that helps the prodigal continue using drugs or alcohol. An addict will care about nothing except getting more substance to abuse. You cannot reason logically with your child while he or she is in this condition.

If your child has an addiction problem, you can expect him or her to lie. As one addict said, "You cannot be a successful addict unless you are a great liar."

And because the only objective in life is getting more drugs, your child may even steal from you or others to support the habit. Your child will end up caring more about getting drugs than about taking your money or heirlooms to get more supplies. If your child is on drugs, feel free to search his or her room frequently for a stash.

Addicts generally will not change until they hit bottom. It's difficult, but showing tough love by asking addicts to leave the home or by calling the police if you find drugs, may in the long run be the most loving thing you can do for your child. As always, don't forget to consider how the child might be affecting other family members. The prodigal's bad choices shouldn't be paid for by your other children or by your marriage.

When Abuse Strikes

The first time George's daughter Shannon wanted to return home, he let her, hoping he could help her. But the next time Shannon wanted to return home, George said no.

"While at home the previous time, Shannon beat her mother and sister," George said. "She'd get into fights with them and soon her fists would be flailing. When Shannon was on drugs or drunk, she was even worse. But even when she wasn't abusing substances, she would often start after those two. If I was home, I'd get her off whomever she was attacking, but even then, Shannon was difficult to control physically. Even though her mother is a larger woman than Shannon, Shannon is much stronger."

Despite the wealth of information on the Internet regarding parenting issues, it's nearly impossible to find advice for parents of children who abuse them. This happens much more often than we'd like to think.

One mother who's also a counselor notes that rebellious behavior, and especially violent behavior, may be a partial result of physical problems. So you might get the child to a doctor and have him or her checked accordingly, as well as setting an appointment with a counselor. You may even visit a psychiatrist who can do both a mental and physical evaluation.

"Learn restraining holds," says Kim, who has had her share of scratches and bruises inflicted by her child. "This can be especially pertinent for people who deal with adopted and foster children, as well as families with natural children who are prodigals.

"I've been to several support groups in which people have admitted that their children have physically attacked them. It's like the secret humiliation none of us ever mentions."

If your child is abusing you physically, no matter how embarrassed you are, tell someone. Show a friend the scratches and bruises while they're fresh. Talk to a counselor or minister. And keep a written log. As we all know, lying usually accompanies prodigal behaviors. At some point, your child may claim you are abusing him or her. You may need to be able to prove that you are the person being abused.

Though it may seem to be a drastic thing to do, the solution, as with illegal behaviors, may be to call the police, especially if the child is over 18. After all, in any case of child abuse or spousal abuse, victims are encouraged to phone the police. Why shouldn't we seek safety in this way if our children are abusing us? Perhaps we fear authorities won't believe that a normal-sized teenager can beat up an adult. Unfortunately, many have seen it before.

As we've mentioned before, ignoring problems doesn't make them go away. An abusive child, just as an abusive adult, is likely to continue abusing and become more violent. If we allow a child to get by with this kind of behavior, we are enabling him or her. He or she will become worse not only toward us but also toward others. Reporting the prodigal may also help him or her face the fact that he or she has some serious issues and needs help.

Again, Take Care of Yourself

Candace isn't quite sure when the normal teen issues and challenges crossed the line, but she does remember the day she realized that their family had a problem. "Tina had sassed me yet again," she remembers. "She always knew exactly what to say to get me furious. I told her if she was going to act like a child, she deserved to be spanked like a child. I had no intentions of spanking her, but then Tina taunted, 'Oh yeah? You can't touch me.'

"Of course I said 'You think so?' and picked her up by the edge of her sweat pants and sweatshirt and put her on her bed. The next thing I knew, this slight 16-year-old was pummeling the life out of me and scratching my hands, arms, and face.

"I finally pinned her arms against the bed, but then she began furiously kicking me in the stomach and chest with jack-rabbit kicks."

The next day, Candace realized some things had to change. "I was at work. I'd worn a suit that covered my arms and a turtleneck shirt to cover the scratches and bruises. But I could still feel them. Breathing was even a bit painful. I knew that Tina had some anger issues. But at that point, I realized I could no longer pretend the problems were going to get better, or that it was just normal teen stuff. I had to face that we had some serious problems."

Candace was working in L.A. at a job she liked, but the commute was a killer. She decided that since she couldn't quit working, she'd have to alleviate some of the stress. She realized she needed a break. She couldn't expect to keep up with her normal pressures and schedule while dealing with a wayward teenager who was dishing out the tough stuff. "I got a job 10 minutes from home and just in the nick of time," she says. "From that point, Tina went from bad to worse. She was involved in drugs, sex, and a few other things. No way could I have dealt with the difficulties at home if I'd still had that job."

As we've mentioned in other chapters, at times parents just need to take care of themselves. When we're dealing with a teenager who has gone astray, especially one who is involved in these really tough issues, it takes every single bit of resolve, courage, and energy to get through it. Do not feel guilty if you have to back off of extracurricular events or responsibilities. Our lives only have so much space in them. Get rid of as many of the stress points as you can to protect yourself from emotional overload. Finally, frequent prayer, asking the Holy Spirit for direction, is the best way to take care of yourself and your family.

Follow Your Own Conscience

"Shauna was 17 when she got pregnant for the first time," Sandy says. "She gave that baby up for adoption. She was into drugs and sleeping with a lot of different men and was soon pregnant again. But this time, Shauna wanted an abortion. I tried to talk her out of it but had no luck."

As if that wasn't enough, Shauna wanted Sandy to go with her. "I debated about it for days," Sandy recalls. "I knew that an unborn baby is a human. I'd grieved over my first grandchild being placed into another home where she'd never know me. I knew that abortion was killing a child, but I couldn't talk Shauna out of it. And she begged me to go, saying she was scared and didn't want to be alone."

Finally, Sandy gave in even though she was acting against her convictions. "That was the worst mistake I've ever made,"

Sandy says. "The nurse told us it was a little girl. And for 12 years, I dealt with incessant guilt and depression over participating in the act that took her little life. So many nights I cried myself sick. But I carried the grief alone. I wouldn't tell a soul, and my daughter never talked about it either. When that little granddaughter would have been entering her teen years, I asked God to forgive me and to comfort me. I asked my daughter to forgive me. At long last we were able to cry together and to grieve over that precious little girl."

As Sandy learned the hard way, no matter what our prodigal is going through, no matter what poor decisions a prodigal has made, we parents have to act according to our own convictions and consciences.

Like Sandy, Anne's prodigal daughter, Gloria, became pregnant at 17. Gloria decided to put her child up for adoption but then battled that decision.

"She was so confused and lost," Anne explains. "We had the parents all chosen, they had the nursery ready. And then Gloria backed out a few weeks before the delivery. She was living at home and asked me to help support her and the baby."

Like Sandy, Anne spent some agonized days thinking and praying about that grandchild. "God had put on my heart that adoption was the best way," Anne remembers. "What a dilemma! I was so torn. In the end I told Gloria that she'd have to go it alone; I couldn't rescue her.

"When the baby was born, she had problems and ended up in an incubator. Gloria wondered if the baby was being punished because of Gloria's sin. She was very confused, but she decided in the end to follow through on her commitment and gave the adoptive parents the gift of her child."

Although it's hard to put your convictions ahead of your child, you have to be able to live with yourself long past the momentary crisis. And it might be something God uses to work in your child's life. When Anne stood firm on her convictions, she was rewarded by Gloria's right decision. Would Sandy's daughter, Shauna, have gone through with the abortion if Sandy had stood firm on her convictions and refused to accompany Shauna? That's one of the things Sandy agonized about for years. She feels Shauna probably would have had the abortion anyway, but Sandy encourages other parents to not put themselves through what she went through.

Many parents can relate to you when your teen goes astray. But if you're one who has faced the really tough stuff with your child like the things mentioned in this chapter—and perhaps even tougher things—you may feel like fewer people understand or can relate to you. And you might be right. Fortunately, a lot of prodigals come back to the Lord and their families before they get into addictions, legal problems, health issues, and the highest-risk behaviors.

The next time you feel alone, think about this father:

- He watched one of his sons kill another one of his sons. Their names were Cain and Abel.

- He saw the son he called "the man after his own heart" not only commit adultery but also try to cover it up with murder. That son, David, watched his own family become a mess of incest, murder, and hatred more salacious than any soap opera plot!

- He watched other children of His lie, steal, kill, hate, become overtaken by rebellion, and pull every other sin in the book.

And He survived. He loved. He continued to laugh and live. With His strength, wisdom, and understanding, you, too, can survive. And love. And continue to laugh and live.

For Your Reflection

- What's the toughest stuff your prodigal has been into? Were you expecting this or was it a complete surprise?

- If you suspect your prodigal is getting into some of the "tough stuff" behavior, how will you deal with it? What is your plan of action?

- What can you do to "de-stress" your life a bit so you have more emotional energy for dealing with your child?

- Think of what your child is like right now. Can you find a parallel in the Bible? How did God respond to this one in scripture?

- Study Heb. 4:9-16. What kind of hope does it give us?

- Write a prayer to God. Tell Him what is on your heart about the child you both love so much.

As Good as It Gets

How long does it take for most teens who have gone astray to come to their senses?

Unfortunately, there are no "average prodigal" statistics. Some kids get a taste of that life and turn around in a matter of days. Some go decades and never "get it."

Like Lisa.

Shelly's eyes and personality gradually shift from vivacious to tired as she talks about her daughter, Lisa. Lisa was the sweetest, happiest, most loving child until she reached her teens. Gradually she morphed into a poster child for rebellion.

"We did all the things parents are supposed to do," Shelly explains. But Lisa seemed determined to destroy her life. At 16, Lisa was pregnant. The baby was born in a world before crisis pregnancy centers and an emphasis on adoption services. Shelly hoped motherhood would have a sobering effect on Lisa. It didn't. The drugs, wild living, and irresponsibility continued. Shelly eventually adopted her first granddaughter to raise as her own child.

The years passed. Lisa never changed. "She became a master manipulator and learned how to work every system there is," Shelly says with a defeated shrug. "And she still does that today."

Rather than keeping steady jobs, Lisa is on a first-name basis with every shelter in the city. She's given a hard-luck story to about half of the churches in their large city. She's even learned the best street corners for panhandling. Shelly tonelessly explains that her firstborn has no pride and no conscience.

As Good as It Gets?

At various times over the years, Shelly thought things might change. At times Lisa expressed a desire to do better, even an eager spiritual repentance. But no true life-change has ever occurred. And now in her late 40s, Lisa appears to be a permanent prodigal.

"I wish 20 years ago, when we were only a few years into this thing, that someone had taught me not to waste all of my time and energy hoping," Shelly levels. "So many times Lisa would briefly 'get religion' or experience something that made her vow she'd change."

Shelly pushes her auburn hair back from her forehead. "I'd get caught up in her promises and would believe her, would get excited, would once again drop everything and everyone else in my life to focus on Lisa. But sure enough, Lisa would quickly revert. She couldn't be bothered with getting her life together."

Lisa still occasionally makes sweeping vows to change, and even changes her ways for a couple of weeks. But Shelly no longer gets excited or feels a surge of hope.

"I don't even care anymore," she explains flatly. "I say 'Good for you.' But I don't believe her. I've come to the realization over the years that this may be as good as it gets with Lisa. I wish someone had told me that years ago. I have to move on with my life."

Being somewhat detached isn't easy, Shelly admits. Lisa has custody of two more young sons who aren't cared for and are left alone for hours, sometimes even a few days, while Lisa pursues her own interests. But Shelly just doesn't have the energy or heart to raise two more young children, even these precious grandsons. Fortunately, she finds that God seems to bring others into their lives who can help them: her parents, Lisa's younger sister, even the daughter Lisa birthed and Shelly raised.

Although Shelly loves her daughter, she advises parents that sometimes for their own sanity they have to give up the hope or expectation that the child will ever change. They have to learn to cope with life as it is.

As Bad as It Gets

Jeri Lyn is another parent who reminds us of the stark reality that all prodigal stories don't have happy endings.

"My second of four children got into drugs, alcohol, and sexual promiscuity at the age of 14 or 15," Jeri Lyn reflects. "He ran away from home at 16 to a Christian minister's home, but that didn't help much. Finally, he got his GED and went into the Air Force."

Before Joel even left for boot camp, he learned that he was going to be a dad. He continued with his Air Force training, but the Air Force wasn't a good place for Joel, either. He was stationed in Germany where drugs and alcohol were even more readily available. He married the mother of his baby girl shortly before his daughter was born.

"That marriage ended in a bitter divorce," Jeri Lyn explains. "He married two more times. The last one could have been his salvation, as the girl was a Christian. But he married her without legally divorcing his second wife. She had left after two months of marriage and moved to Texas with a previous boyfriend. My son didn't know how to get in touch with her, though that's not an excuse. Shortly after his third marriage,

Joel received divorce papers from his second wife that were sent to our house. She wanted to marry her boyfriend since they had two kids together. My son signed the papers, but also told his wife. She left him and filed for an annulment."

Joel's life went from bad to worse. "After a 16-year-old girl rejected him, my 32-year-old son committed suicide," she says, tears filling her eyes. "Such a tragic waste of life. He was Mr. Personality and had all kinds of people trying to get him on the right track. He simply made all the wrong choices. As his mother, I begged, prayed, and intervened as often as I could. Yet no one could persuade him that life could be lived without deadening oneself to the pain.

"It's 11 years now since he took his life," Jeri Lyn says, looking down at her hands. "I still miss him," she whispers.

The Reality of Hope

Sometimes the unwanted job of parenting a prodigal is a lifetime task. As Shelly suggests, realizing early that this may be as good as it gets keeps us stable, avoiding the continual roller coaster ride of hope and despair for decades.

But for so many parents and prodigals, the long season of rebellion and irresponsible behavior eventually fades. Thank God that the message most parents of prodigals give is one of hope.

Angie first started down the prodigal road by stealing when she was 13. Before long she was sneaking out of the house to meet guys. Drugs and promiscuity quickly entered the picture.

"I had some hope when she started attending a Christian college," her mom, Pat, says. "But it was short-lived. I realized that although Angie had agreed to attend a Christian college, she hadn't changed. And instead, the nightmares increased. Angie started calling us from college, talking about suicide.

"Ps. 126 became my source of strength. Bill and Gloria Gaither wrote a song—'Joy Comes in the Morning' is the title, I think. I sang it over and over again as I prayed for our lost daughter."

Unfortunately, before the end of the college year, Angie had quit college, moved out of her dorm and in with a boyfriend. "He offered her a dream," Pat says. "He had money. He had position. He promised happiness. Angie believed him."

The nightmare got worse. For a year and a half, Pat and her husband, Joe, had no idea where Angie was. They only had a post office box for her. "Once in a while she called, but months went by when we didn't hear anything. I'd wake up in a sweat wondering if this guy drugged our daughter or if he was a pimp. Fear of losing our firstborn drove me to my knees."

Years passed before Pat and Joe saw Angie again. The church Joe pastored held a surprise party for the couple and flew Angie home. "It was a happy reunion," Pat recalls. But still, Angie was running spiritually and emotionally. Seven years passed before Angie visited home again.

"Angie had been in beauty pageants, and when she got off the plane others saw her beauty; I saw her pain-filled eyes and frozen face until we arrived home," Pat explains. "That's when the fun began. Stories of family, remembrances of old times, and her three-year-old niece's antics made Angie laugh until she cried. We could see that her heart was softening. Angie stayed for a week and even sang praise songs with us on a family trip. I hoped she'd remember the scriptures she'd learned as a child too.

"That was February. In the middle of a night in July, the Lord cracked the last wall. Angie asked God to forgive her and called her sister. Her sister drove across state to move Angie out of the house she was living in with her boyfriend.

"Today, that same daughter is a beautiful woman: a wife and mother, a leader in her church, an encouraging counselor and my good friend. The prodigal returned to the Father."

It's Not Over Until . . .

For Jan, hope came with a change in focus. Until that point, her daughter, Sue, looked hopeless. At 14, Sue started abusing drugs when her father abandoned the family.

"I had her in several teen programs—a residential program, a remote ranch for troubled teens, Teen Challenge. She bolted from all of them. She was involved in everything from promiscuity to drugs to abortion to living on the street to Satan worship. I sent her to Tough Love programs, read a zillion books, and researched more programs."

Jan was at the end of her rope when God began to nudge her own heart. "I used to call Sue my 'prodigal,'" Jan says. "But then God urged me to begin seeing her as His child instead of as my prodigal rebel. That made all the difference. I started seeing her as He did—a lovely child of God with promise and with purpose. That changed everything. I still depended on prayer support from my friends, and I still made a strong stand, even packing her bags for her to leave when she wouldn't abide by my rules. I even sent her to jail when she and her friends stole from me.

"But I began to look beyond the way she appeared at the time and tried to see the finished product, a woman after God's own heart, and it gave me peace. My friends couldn't believe how I started responding to Sue and her problems. When I made the decision to see her as the finished product, I stopped panicking and being depressed. I chose hope. It was the only way I could survive—the evidence was so bleak and she was so messed up.

"But she couldn't outrun God. I thought she hit bottom

when she got pregnant and gave up the child for adoption, but it proved not to be. I wondered what would happen next, as most of us do. But a few more battles and losses and she was ready to go back to what she knew. She reached out to the Lord and He was there. She's never been the same since. Now, at 29, she is a changed woman, a committed Christian.

"It's amazing," Jan says with an awed smile. "She's healed of the guilt, anger, and bitterness and tells her story to everyone. What a witness!

And there are so many more stories just like these.

"My son Rob became a prodigal when he was 16 years old," Elena says. "He drank away 15 years of his life after he graduated from high school. I prayed for God to help him bottom out and seek help. He finally did and has now been in alcoholic recovery for 14 years. Two years after he hit bottom, he fulfilled his lifelong dream of becoming a commercial artist, marrying, and now has two lovely children. He's very much a nurturing, fatherly person."

Preparing for the Feast

As most parents of teenagers who have gone astray have discovered, the prodigal life includes travel time. Your child might have taken a few years to reach the "pigpen," and it may take him or her a few years to get home. After all, any journey we take physically requires time to get from one point to another, usually with many stops and rests along the way. The same can be true for emotional and spiritual journeys.

During the first few years while Nick was a prodigal, his mom, Paula, tried to gain control of the situation in every way she knew how. She tried "guilting" her son off the sinful path, tried manipulation, tried unconditional love, tried everything. Finally, God told her to stop everything and only pray.

"During those days of praying, I was teaching an adult class in Sunday School and we were in the books of Kings and Chronicles. The prophet had come before God and was laying out his case for God's people. He acknowledged that they had done wrong and deserved whatever judgment God would mete out to them. But, he pleaded with God to temper that judgment with His infinite mercy and to be only as severe with them as He had to be to turn them to repentance.

"This is the prayer God showed me to pray for our son, 'God, he is so far from You and walking in all the wrong places and making all the wrong choices. He deserves punishment. But would You be as merciful as You can be, but as severe as You have to be to get his attention. I trust You with Your child, my son.'"

One morning during church, Nick slipped into the seat beside Paula. "He grabbed my hand and gave it a big squeeze. That started a long walk back to our home, and he's still walking back to his God. He hasn't completely returned to God yet, and we still get those dreaded late-night phone calls, but he's on his way. God hasn't left him or us, and we have the faith that He's finishing what He started in our son's life. One day we'll have a son who walks close to God."

Paula straightens the cuff of her blouse unconsciously as she ponders, "I heard a famous preacher once say that whatever it takes to get us to our knees will always be in our lives to keep us on our knees. Our child drove me to my knees and into a deeper relationship with God than I ever thought possible. My favorite thing to tell other parents dealing with prodigals is this: When my son is completely restored and not only back in our family's fold but also in his Heavenly Father's fold, it will be a wonderful miracle and an answer to my deepest yearning.

"But another miracle will be what God has done in my heart and in my walk with Him. I am light-years ahead of where I was when this started nearly 20 years ago. I have a greater confidence in who God is and what His plan is for my life and the life of my son than I ever could have had without this journey.

Paula especially relates to the story of the prodigal son in the Bible. "We still stand at the door and look down the road, as did the father in Luke 15," she says. "We wait for that phone call that says, 'Mom, God is doing a new work in my life.'

"Meanwhile, we consider it the greatest honor to be in the waiting room with God while He continues to work in the life of our son. And, like the Luke 15 father, we already have the banquet planned and we will sing God's praises every day until it happens. God has proven himself faithful to our family and to our prodigal."

God will be faithful to you, too, no matter what situation you face. From the "this is as good as it gets" that Shelly endured to watching your child on his or her journey, as Paula is experiencing, you can know that you are not alone. Your child is also God's child. He grieves with you, hopes with you, and rejoices with you. And He gives you grace.

But He also steps into your child's life in places you can't go. God walks with your child through the difficult valleys in his or her life. When your child runs away from you emotionally, God brings His message into your child's life through other people. When your child will no longer listen to you—no matter how hard his or her heart—the Holy Spirit can reach into the crevices and convict, reminding your beloved child of the seeds of righteousness you've planted in the past.

Perhaps the words of Ps. 31:24 are the best message we parents of prodigals can carry in our hearts: "Be strong and take heart, all you who hope in the LORD."

For Your Reflection

- Consider that your child is on a journey. Describe where you feel your child is. Is he or she on the way out or on the way back to your home?

- Do you feel your child is closer to being back in your family's fold, or is he or she more likely to return to God before finding peace with you?

- What amusement park attraction best describes your emotional ride with your prodigal?

- If you knew your child would be a prodigal for 20 more years, what would you do differently?

- Contemplate Ps. 126. What verses does God draw you to? Write down what you feel God says to you through this scripture.

- What does James 1:12 say to the parent of the prodigal?

- Memorize Ps. 31:24. May the Holy Spirit bring it to your heart and mind when your courage and faith feel low.

Notes

1. Caryn D. Rivadeneira, "Married with Prodigals," *Marriage Partnership* 17, no. 2 (Summer 2000), 38.

2. Statistics from National Runaway Switchboard web site: www.nrscrisisline.org. National Runaway Switchboard, 3080 N. Lincoln Ave., Chicago, IL 60657 (773-880-9860).

3. Information from National Center for Missing and Exploited Children web site: www.missingkids.org. National Center for Missing and Exploited Children, Charles B. Wang International Children's Building, 699 Prince St., Alexandria, VA 22314-3175 (703-274-3900).

4. National Runaway Switchboard web site: www.nrscrisisline.org. National Runaway Switchboard, 3080 N. Lincoln Ave., Chicago, IL 60657 (773-880-9860).

5. Information from National Center for Missing and Exploited Children web site: www.missingkids.org. National Center for Missing and Exploited Children, Charles B. Wang International Children's Building, 699 Prince St., Alexandria, VA 22314-3175 (703-274-3900).

6. Ibid.

7. Carla Barnhill, "Loving Your Prodigal," *Christian Parenting Today* 12, no. 6 (July/August 2000), 38.

8. David Hertzler, "Good News About Runaway Children," *Today's Native Father* (March/April 2000), issue 108.

9. Ginger Kolbaba, "Finding God Faithful," *Today's Christian Woman* 23, no. 6 (November/December 2001), 62.

10. Barnhill, "Loving Your Prodigal," 38.

11. James Dobson, "Dr. Dobson's Study," www.family.org/docstudy/solid/a0008702.html.

12. Kolbaba, "Finding God Faithful," 62.

13. Barnhill, "Loving Your Prodigal," 38.

14. Kolbaba, "Finding God Faithful," 62.

15. Harold Ivan Smith, "Life After Loss," *Moody Magazine* (July/August 2000), web site archives: www.moodymagazine.com/articles.php?action=view_article&id=427

16. Wesley D. Tracy, "Preventing Spiritual Fatigue," *Moody Magazine* (July/August 2000), web site archives: www.moodymagazine.com/articles.php?action=view_article&id=429

17. www.family.org/pplace/youandteens/a0021601.cfm - 32.0KB - Focus on the Family